MEDIA IN THE CELEBRITY CULTURE SPHERE AND OTHER ESSAYS

BERTHA MKWELELE

Tellwell Talent
www.tellwell.ca

ISBN
978-0-2288-2103-8 (Hardcover)
978-0-2288-2102-1 (Paperback)
978-0-2288-2104-5 (eBook)

DEDICATION

For Neema Edward Mkwelele
for beautiful, overwhelming, glorious,
frightening, endless love.

TABLE OF CONTENTS

ACKNOWLEDGEMENT

*M*any people have encouraged and supported me in countless ways and I am grateful. My thanks go to:

- My husband, Edward, who has been there and always encouraged me.
- My son Michael, who in his own unique way encouraged me by making me laugh when I thought I no longer had it in me.

Neema wrote the essays collected here between 2007 and 2010, a sharply defined period in her life. It was a period of search, reflection and discovery. Nine years later, as the collection is about to be published, it is interesting to note that her discoveries are still relevant.

Neema talked a great deal about her academic work, and her family supported her and her ambition. We, Neema's family, owe a debt of gratitude to the academic institutions and teachers who inspired Neema Edward Mkwelele, especially in Cornwall, United Kingdom. Her university taught her strong academic values so that she might enjoy enhanced knowledge and skills in life, with all of the benefits that would bring.

The problems with media and social networking remain, and more remains to be said about it by other curious and reflective people. Perhaps this collection of Neema's work will be a good reference for them. Safety issues in relation to social media and networking are an especially relevant topic of discussion today. The act of *calling* a safety or security method an enhancement does not actually make it so; using multiple methods simultaneously to achieve appropriate security has greater prospects for net safety.

It is a pleasure to thank my family for their generous encouragement as well as the University of Falmouth in the United Kingdom, whose staff members very helpfully read over all of Neema's essays.

Finally, I wish to express my gratitude to the Neema Edward Mkwelele Wellness Foundation for its existence, which feeds me so that for the first time in my life I wrote a book as I walked my grieving journey.

CHAPTER 1

About Neema Edward Mkwelele

Don't limit a child to your own learning,
for he was born in another time.
– Rabindranath Tagore.

Neema Edward Mkwelele was born in Tanzania on January 5, 1989. Her early education was in Kenya. She went to primary school at St. Lucia Academy in Kinamba; then to Taita Academy in Mwatate; and finally to Bura Girls High School in Bura. When she graduated, she was accepted into Falmouth University, a specialized university for the creative industries based in Falmouth and Penryn, Cornwall, in the United Kingdom. She graduated with a Bachelor of Arts Degree (Honours) in Broadcasting in 2010. Before her graduation, in her second year, she went to study at the Emily Carr University of Art and Design, in Vancouver, British Columbia, Canada as an international exchange program student. This school is a world leader in leading art, design, and media programs. She was preparing to go to Santiago, Chile for a job placement at the time of her death.

Neema was an enthusiastic writer, and had been ever since she was a child. My husband and I helped her at home when she first learned to read and write, but once she mastered the basics, she no longer needed our assistance. As she grew, so did her love for reading, which fostered in her a love for writing.

Neema wrote about every important event in her life, and kept a good number of notebooks. Many of the stories in this book were found in those notebooks. Her writing was inspired by many people, including her parents, friends and teachers—but she was also proudly inspired by her own beautiful name, Neema. Neema is Swahili for 'grace'.

Neema grew up learning and understanding that her name was not only beautiful, but was a special name on Earth according to the Bible. Neema wrote about her understanding of grace and she also remembered the name of the teacher, Mr. Muthana, at Taita Academy Mwatate (her primary school) who taught her about grace. She wrote down what the teacher told her and her fellow students about it, as well as what God said about grace, in one of her many notebooks.

This page is from one of her notebooks when she was at Taita Academy Mwatate primary school.

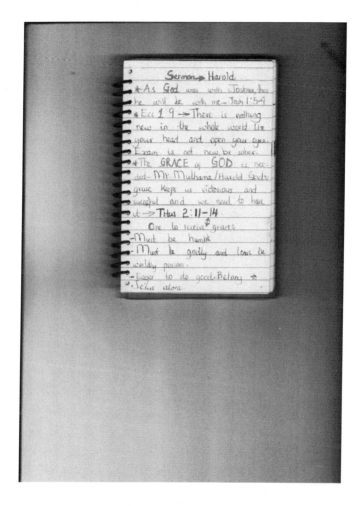

After finishing university, Neema was ready to contribute to the world. She began looking for jobs. Below is her resume.

***

Neema Edward
Email: neema.mkw@gmail.com
Mobile: +447787725232

I am an ambitious and enthusiastic graduate who is inspired by challenge and loves to take initiative to achieve results. I am keen to find a position as a Project Assistant in a communications and media position. I am reliable, trustworthy, competent and always willing to learn new skills.

Education
2007 – 2010: University College Falmouth, UK – BA (HONS) Broadcasting 2:1

- 1st year units: Media Theories, Camera operating and editing skills, Broadcasting methods
- 2nd year units: Documentary making, Broadcasting research methods, Scriptwriting, Radio production
- One semester exchange at Emily Carr University of Art/Design/Media (Canada) studying Film, Video, Integrated Media
- 3rd year units: Project management, Media campaigning, Academic research skills, Dissertation writing, Preproduction, production and post-production skills

2003 – 2006: Bura Girls' High School, Kenya – A levels

- English Literature: A / Biology: A / Chemistry; B / Mathematics: B

Skills

Skilled content creator (blogging, articles) with excellent writing skills

- I have been blogging and creating online content for three years making sure to gain exposure by using social media platforms such Twitter, Facebook and Stumbleupon

IT skills: (Intermediate HTML and CSS, Experienced user of all MS Office components, Intermediate Adobe Photoshop user)

- I utilise these skills by maintaining and updating the Go Girl Magazine Website and my personal blogs.

Media software usage skills (Experienced Pro Tools, Avid, After Effects user)

- Gained experience through undertaking various media production projects at University.

Employment
August 2010 - Present: Go Girl Magazine, Online Travel Magazine – Business Manager

- Identifying potential clients and communicating with them
- Updating website, monitoring and managing the magazine's social networking profiles
- Liaising with advertisers
- Communicating with press and media contacts
- Co-ordinating with the magazine's team of writers on topics to cover
- Research on travel destinations, hotel and travel book reviews

April 2010 – July 2010: Cornwall Hospice Care, UK - Volunteer Shop Assistant

- Cash handling and serving customers behind the till
- Arranging and pricing donated items
- General cleaning and maintaining of the shop

August 2007 – August 2008: Office Angels Recruitment Agency, UK - Office Assistant

- Data entry
- Communications with potential recruits
- General office management

Interests
Travelling

- I have had the opportunity to travel and live in different countries, something which I enjoyed and learnt a lot from in terms of interacting with a variety of people and experiencing how different cultures work. I'm especially drawn to European culture.

Social media and Web design

- I'm a social media enthusiast and use this platform to communicate with people sharing similar interests in music, film and television.

Scriptwriting

- I'm a freelance scriptwriter.

Music, Film and Television

- I enjoy following a diverse range of music, film and television genres and I'm especially keen on reviewing them.

★★★

Neema collapsed at the Gatwick International Airport in London, United Kingdom, and passed away on February 21, 2011. She was only 22 years old.

CHAPTER 2

Why is Neema's Story Important?

In your life you touched so many, in your death many lives were changed

> — *Melinda Jones, independent scholar,*
> *feminist human rights lawyer and*
> *disability advocate.*

I am writing this book for a number of reasons; first and foremost, to answer the question, why is Neema's story important?

On a personal level, losing a child is a universal tragedy, and I hope that by sharing Neema's story and my own grieving journey, in my small way I can help other women who have had similar experiences with their own grief. Also, I can truly say that Neema's life and death changed my life, and my family's as well. Her death helped me discover my passion, one I did know I had. Because of losing Neema, I decided to get directly involved with advocacy work. Her death prompted the formation of the Neema Foundation, which advocates for the education of African girls. (https://www.neemaedwardmkwelelewellnessfoundation.org)

I am happy to do what I am doing from the bottom of my heart because I believe that when you're passionate about what you do, you do everything well. The Mkwelele family have decided to pay tribute to Neema and her legacy in this very special way. We have dedicated ourselves to changing other people's lives, particularly vulnerable girls in poor Tanzania. This work gives us purpose and has helped us understand the value of human life. My family believes God has called us to do this work; incredibly, after hearing His voice, we pulled together to create the foundation. It wasn't easy, but we have done our best and we have dedicated our lives to her memory since the day she left us to be with the Lord. She would be so proud. I only wish we were there to say goodbye when she left this Earth.

The Mkwelele family—Neema's family—is optimistic that the Neema Foundation will be able to join with other organizations and people who are doing their best to protect children from violence, abuse, neglect, and poor treatment. The work we are involved in goes beyond honoring our beautiful daughter, and the foundation is the vehicle to carry out some of Neema's higher dreams about equality and safety for all. This work will make a difference in other people's lives. Many girls in Tanzania will benefit from the work of the Neema Foundation. Simply put, the Neema Foundation is about honouring the example Neema set.

The fund-raising the non-profit Neema Foundation does is totally dedicated to helping African youth at risk, particularly Tanzanian girls. We believe this is what Neema would want to see—girls and other youth from the country of her birth benefitting and being offered the opportunities that she was fortunate enough to have.

I strongly believe that everyone can be an advocate for children and we can create a world where they can be safe and happy.

CHAPTER 3

What about Bertha?

I was born in Tanzania, raised in Tanzania, worked in Tanzania (my husband and I worked in the finance industry) and I raised my two children in Tanzania. And I like travelling! When my children were old enough to be on their own, I travelled abroad to pursue further studies in other countries, including the United Kingdom.

As a mother, I am so thankful that God blessed me with two wonderful children, my daughter Neema and her younger brother, Michael. I have enjoyed my children from day one and delighted in watching them grow. While I was in the United Kingdom, my children came to visit during their holidays and we had some amazing and meaningful travelling experiences. After Neema completed her secondary education (in Kenya), she decided to move to the United Kingdom and she took her Bachelor of Arts degree at the University of Falmouth in Cornwall. Cornwall is in the southwest and it is one of the most beautiful areas in United Kingdom.

As a Christian, I believe God wants us to do what we love, and love what we do—and to work for him.

Sometimes small things make a difference in other people's lives, or even just brighten their day, and we should take steps to do such things for others.

I believe Neema loved what she did while she was with us here on Earth; she travelled to foreign countries to do what she loved to do and got to see some of the world before her untimely death. She enjoyed and loved what she did for the people around her, and she acted with kindness because God asked her to do so. She did the things she did, and she loved what she was doing, to glorify him.

My personal experience tells me that when we do what God asks us to do, and love what we do, we never fall short of love. It's incredible; God made it so. If you love what you do, love will find you even when you are not with us here on Earth. Yes, my daughter Neema loved what she did, and love still follows her even though she is no longer with us. The evidence is clear, because the Neema Foundation is shining and doing well. That is how I know that love is following Neema.

The work that we do with the Neema Foundation is legacy work. I am proud of what we are doing in our Neema's name. It's my family's joy to see and know that her death is having a positive impact on many children and girls. God is great. It is true that when one door closes, another opens. I did not want to lose my daughter and I experienced great pain when she died. But if she had not died, the Neema Foundation would not exist.

My story is a moving one and I hope it will inspire all women who have lost a child, or children. I am optimistic that some of these women might reach out to me and consider joining or volunteering for the Neema Foundation. Your precious child may be gone, but there are so many others in the world who need help. In my country, Tanzania, we help girls in remote, rural areas to get an education. That is the root of a strong, peaceful world; educated children.

I strongly believe that children around the world will benefit from the Neema Foundation project. Through our outreach efforts, poor children in Tanzania will get an opportunity to be educated and other children around the world will get an opportunity to have a unique, life-changing experience through service opportunities organized through the Neema Foundation.

I am going to repeat myself here: **I strongly believe that through the Neema Foundation, many children, youth and students around the world will travel to Tanzania (rural and remote areas of the country) for an unforgettable service-learning trip that will change how they see the world.**

CHAPTER 4

Neema's Portfolio

> *I have worked on the vital task of collecting, organizing and collating Neema's portfolio, which she left behind for her family to treasure.*
>
> **– Bertha Mkwelele**

*W*alking into the house after Neema's funeral, I was struck by emptiness, by the enormity of the loss of my first child and my only daughter. Inside me, a voice was talking to me, asking why this had happened. Before the funeral, I maintained an illusion that my daughter was still in the world. It was only after the burial that I started to really understand that she was never coming back. Life looked me up and down and shook every part of my body until finally I said this to myself, "I feel bolder now." I had swum in the depths of grieving and loss; nothing could be worse. Surviving it had released me from fear I had been victimized by all my life. I realized I could learn a lot of new things. And this is how the Neema Foundation was born.

Neema wanted to be a travel writer; that was her career choice. Why do have to tell the whole world?

Because after finishing high school Neema worked hard to get to the bottom of what she wanted to do, and it was not easy because there are so many choices in today's world. Many young people, including Neema, struggle with this big challenge, and feel overwhelmed and also dark. To find a clear path is sometimes very frightening. But Neema was more fortunate than most in that she knew she was going to be a writer her entire life. This is why she made that choice and also why she worked so hard on her writing skills. She was also very fortunate to have such excellent instruction and I would like to acknowledge the loving dedication her instructors at Falmouth University and Emily Carr University contributed to the shaping of her writing skills. It helped make Neema the insightful young woman that she was.

A number of psychology researchers have raised this question: Why are so many young people overwhelmed by today's possibilities? Gary Bernhard, Ed.D. and Kalman Glantz, Ph.D. propose that, with so many options, the possibility of making wrong choices can be paralyzing for some and they get overwhelmed and confused by all the options life presents, which produces angst. Why are they not delighted by all the possibilities? Probably some are, but research indicates that is not the norm.

Some social psychologists say young people thrive on trying out new things, having new experiences, and experiencing different styles of education. Creative teaching styles can be an extremely important element of the teaching process in higher education, as can improving curricula. Further, if young people can be assessed for their preferred learning style, then they can make meaningful choices about their education. This would let them more easily get in touch with what they actually enjoy doing, and what makes them feel like they're making a valuable contribution to family and community.

I think parents, educators, and therapists should understand that many young people are less interested in being all they can be than they are in finding something to do that has meaning.

My incredible, amazing daughter, Neema was only in the universe for a short time, but she knew exactly what she wanted. She also knew the path to get it at very young age. Neema was one of the lucky ones, for a Tanzanian female. She was born in secure, middle class family, had access to education and could make plans to go to broadcasting school, unlike many other girls of her age. She dreamed of an exciting career in the media and entertainment industry, and of living and working as travel writer. Neema's strength was that she wrote in her own, unique 'young person' voice, and at only 22 years old, she was determined. She seemed to be telling herself, 'I am doing some great work' and she lived by that, with confidence. The two universities Neema attended contributed immensely to Neema's success and I am grateful she had the opportunity to attend them.

She was so young when she died, and I think there were many voices and questions about her future in her mind. One of voices was saying, "I am at the beginning, I am young and such a stranger to myself, and I hardly exist," And another was saying, "I must go out into the world and see it, and hear it, and react to it, before I know at all who I am and what I want to be." She did not shy away from this; she wanted to share her values with the world.

Unfortunately, things did not work out that way.

I can hear her voice as I write this sentence (I find myself making a mental note to dance a little when I get home), just as I can hear how she would have delivered to the world the dialogue in her plays, or read aloud from the essays collected in this book.

Neema reflected on her image, as a young person and as a girl, and had the ability to lose herself in the beauty and mystery of both the natural world and the world of writing. Each word she left behind is precious to me, including everything in the following selected essays. The essays have not been chosen by personal preference about the various subjects; rather, they speak to my enduring loss and eternal attachment to the person who wrote them. As I navigated the dark corridors of the path of hidden grieving, on this extremely difficult journey I found myself and my family clinging to God as we built a new life. God's all-knowing power seems to change all things. Life is change. And life is good.

Until we started the Neem Foundation, I was living pointless, shapeless days that weren't bringing me any closer to anything. For the first time in my life, I couldn't think of anything I particularly wanted to do. Nothing blossomed for me or seemed extraordinary in my life anymore, nor would anything ever happen the same way again. I wondered about Neema and who she would have become if she had lived. All I had left was her essays, and they were calling to me. I got the idea of doing something with them, of putting together a beautiful piece of academic work.

This collection of Neema's essays and other written work contains a discussion of the power of the media, especially online media; analysis of methods of communication; and, some critical reviews of television arts, among other things. Though Neema is not with us physically, this is wealth sharing on her behalf. I think it is important to continue the discussion about the role of media in shaping societal behaviour and attitudes, especially attitudes of people toward one another.

Putting this collection of essays out into the world is my way of continuing the discussion, my way of re-birthing my brilliant daughter in a manner that can help others as she would have, had she lived. I believe there are profoundly different ways in which we can have relationships with others, and we shape those relationships. My hope is that through this book—the second book I have written about Neema—the reader can have a relationship of sorts with Neema and be inspired by how efficiently she used her short time in the universe. Her career path shaped her into the person she was; a person with good character who was passionate, vibrant, intelligent, and loving.

These essays are more than academic materials; they are part of an interesting discussion about topics and characters that fit well with social issues in every society. She wrote very entertaining stories and demonstrated a clear understanding of the relationship between the career she was in (the media), people, service providers and users and society in general. She was able to explain the core responsibility and role of the media, and she touched on the challenges of disseminating information in a meaningful way, as well as why this is so important.

Safety and security when using social media creates moral, political and economic agendas that do not always favor service users. A consistent commitment to safety and security is important, and ethical features that begin with one person or industry radiate outward toward others. Media and the entertainment industry should model appropriate behaviour.

This raises the question: Is what is being done is good enough? This is a challenge for our time. It's troubling effectively monitor information dissemination by mass media. Their policies and agendas shape the information that is transmitted, as well as what is perceived in the public sphere. In the same way, celebrities shape social structure, using social media, in the cultural sphere. I form my own opinions, as Neema did, but many are influenced by readily available online information, no matter how accurate it is.

Neema's essays highlight the importance of getting to know the process of how we receive information. In her work, Neema discusses the relationship between the media and the audience, as well as the type of information presented. She wrote that the media presents topics for targeted audiences based on profiling. Facebook is one example of social media that profiles its users and targets advertisements toward them. For advertisers, identifying specific pages with high engagement is important because it gives them the opportunity to present topics that are relevant to the audience of that page. It's a fascinating process.

After studying Neema's work, I see the world differently, with fresher eyes. When I look at her written works and think about the person who wrote them, I know her perspectives have influenced my own. I have added her name to my 'influenced by' list, and I am proud that my daughter is one of the people who's wisdom and insight has influenced me over the years.

Because I had a lot of unanswered questions about the things Neema wrote, I did some research about the media to get more insight. Questions I wanted to answer included:

- What was on her mind when she wrote the essays?
- What major challenges did she face?
- What influenced the choice of the topics she wrote about?
- What influenced the choice of the characters she wrote about?
- What led her to pick those characters?

And finally:

- What was her relationship with people around her at the particular time when she was writing?

As her mother, I wonder about who, or what, influenced her. I wonder about her relationship with her classmates, roommates, fellow students, lecturers, faculty members and neighbours at the university she attended. She was growing into a well-versed academic and a strong woman when she died. Who was surrounding her? Who was the family she created when she left her birth family behind?

This is what I want to tell you about my Neema: When she wrote her essays, she took into consideration *all* of her surroundings—the university environment and the students, lecturers and staff members, as well as the local people and their culture. All of it influenced her. She attended University College of Falmouth in South West England, and she loved it there. It was an excellent university and she seemed to easily be able to establish relationships with people in the country she was living in. Her selection of writing topics was predominantly about herself and her ability to make relationships work. I interpret her stories to be about how, as a Tanzanian citizen, she integrated so well into a new country. She was able to learn about people and understand their culture. She was also able to allow people into her life; she gave them the opportunity to learn about her too.

It was a good move for a young woman of Neema's age to go to England, and many of the characters in the things she liked to read and write about were English, no doubt because she lived there. For example, in the case study she did about celebrity lifestyle and culture, she chose an English celebrity named Kerry Katona. Using this woman's public persona as an example, she examined the relationship between the media and the entertainment industry with an eye to how celebrities use social media in the context of business marketing.

What I learned from reading this case study is that media and the entertainment industry work hand in hand and sometimes share common goals. When they make decisions to act collaboratively, they can form ethical partnerships for the common good—for example, when celebrities endorse programs that raise money or donate in other ways to the needy. Before I collected and read Neema's essays, I did not know the significance of this. Neema wrote about the times in which we live.

I believe Neema's essays are as relevant today as they were when she wrote them, if not more so. The challenges around monitoring and controlling social media and online activities, including private information sharing, are getting worse, particularly for vulnerable people who are easily conned. This is a continuous challenge and problem for us all. The trend is getting bigger as new types of social media are introduced. Neema argued that the media has both power and responsibility. I agree, because I believe user safety and security should be prioritized by the industry. User safety is vital. The success of media and entertainment companies should be gauged on how safe they are for their users. Strict security measures should be required for online activities, especially private information sharing. A company that invests in social media should be obligated to protect its members and service users, so they are not placed in jeopardy.

They should ensure safety and security, and right-based action.

A number of researchers have pointed out that more work is needed, and argued that there is a need to do things differently and change our mentality around social media. By doing this, we can stay safe while we enjoy online activities. Some efforts have been made to improve safety and security, but I have heard about some significant safety breaches. For example, *Scientific American,* in the article, *Industry Roundtable: Improving Online Security (Extended version),* August 18, 2008, described efforts that have been made to improve things. The article says security professionals are calling for upgraded technology, along with more attention to human and legal factors, to protect against numerous, sophisticated attacks by hackers. The article talked about the future of online security, and tried to predict the picture in ten years.

Ten years later, on February 1, 2019, Neil J. Rubenking and Jill Duffy wrote in *PC MAG* about few simple steps you can follow to protect the security of your data and online identity. The article is called *12 Simple Things You Can Do to Be More Secure Online.* These steps included installing antivirus software and keeping it updated, exploring the security tools you install, using unique passwords for every login, getting a VPN and learning how to use it, using two factor authentication, using passcodes even when they are optional, and paying securely with your smartphone.

Since online security breaches are becoming more common, these incidents and online activities made me think of Neema and her essays. People have lots of good ideas and want to share them, but I would encourage each and one of you to sit still for a minute and think about what you can do to be safer online. I think our mentality is the same today as when the essays were written and I also think online safety and security have not changed much. Media companies still do things the way they always have.

In my opinion, both the media and the entertainment industries need to invest more in staff training which would allow staff members to understand and communicate more effectively with different cultures. I also think that they need to have open minds, meaning that something unusual will always happen, and they need to be able to anticipate the unexpected. They need to be proactive instead of reactive when it comes to online security.

All companies need to train employees in each area of security, especially in risky areas. Trained employees should be equipped with knowledge, skills and ability to minimize incidents and avoid security breaches. Very highly trained employees should specialize in issues such as online bullying and harassment. In her writing, Neema pointed how online bullying impacts young people, affecting their quality of life and creating personal struggles as they grow from youth to adulthood.

There are many online resources that can guide a person about how to stay safe and enjoy online activities. Most of the information people need is available online, but companies should offer information specific to their own products. This will keep people engaged as they learn how to do online activities safely. No one is 100 percent sure where to get the help they need, and you never know what you're going to encounter when you post your personal information online, particularly sensitive personal information such as banking details.

There is a growing call to continue discussing safety and security issues on the web. I think it's time we work together to reduce the risks and to keep online activities safe and secure. Sometimes this means saving lives.

Incredibly, analyzing Neema's essays showed me that many of the same security issues are haven't changed since she wrote her papers a decade ago. Maybe in our time the situation will improve. Certainly people now understand the basics of online safety and security, including supervising children online, not giving personal information out and working on secured networks.

Invasion of privacy was a problem a decade ago, and it still is. As I pointed out earlier, though the situation has improved, more needs to be done. While much brainstorming has occurred to find better ways of sharing information safely, the problem remains. More needs to be done with social media operations like Facebook and Twitter as well as in the online business and marketing sector. Perhaps this collection of Neema's written academic work about social media and online information sharing will help continue the dialogue about this profound challenge and social issue.

It is a pleasure to have the opportunity to publish Neema's work. It is a way to thank her for her remarkable insight. Her erudition made her very special. She connected with many people, including her lecturers at the two universities she attended. Some of her former professors very helpfully read her essays and authenticated the collection, which I am grateful for. And I find I the impertinent energy and wit of this young woman, Neema—my daughter— more precious in her absence as I read them.

The most important of Neema's documents that I have published in this book is her dissertation, *Media in the Celebrity Culture Sphere*. According to Neema, information has great power, thus the media—a key transmitter of information—wields great power. Timely information is vital for humankind to keep us plugged into the culture in which we live, as well as to keep people informed about such things as the recent pandemic.

Celebrity culture is much the same. People live vicariously through celebrities and the media keeps them plugged into the nuances of particular celebrities' lives. Neema wrote about Kerry Katona in her dissertation, and how the media turned on her and vilified her when once she had been glorified. To be clear, Neema wrote about Kerry Katona not because she loved celebrity culture, but because understood the power of the media and thought examination of its fickle nature was in order. She gave her perspectives and encouraged others to start a dialogue about the relationship between the media and celebrities as well.

I did a Google search and found an article (on Jezebel.com) called *The 19th Century Queen of Celebrity Culture*, by Kelly Faircloth. Kelly wrote about Columbia University English Professor Sharon Marcus' book, *The Drama of Celebrity*. In it, she examines Sarah Bernhardt, an actress who died in 1923, who is credited as being the first woman to manipulate the media to her own advantage. Marcus explains it as a kind of meta-theater. "Celebrity is this alchemy of interactions between publics, media, and the stars themselves, and you can't really predict who's going to be a star, who's going to stay a star—and that itself, I came to realize, is part of why we're interested in celebrities. We're not just interested in celebrities because we like knowing about who's divorcing whom and whether someone got rid of her baby bump quickly. We're also interested in how our own interest is going to pan out."

The celebrity culture sphere is a perfect example to use when discussing the power of the media in shaping ideas, which can control otherwise free societies. Neema used a case study about celebrity culture to explore the contribution of social media to the relationships between media itself, celebrity and society and to tell her audiences what it means to be a celebrity. It has implications for everyone.

I think Neema and Sharon Marcus have similar perspectives. Says Marcus, "There's an unpredictable gaming element to it, and we're one of the players, but we're not the only player." That's what makes celebrity culture compelling. Further, ongoing business implications are brought to the fore. Media conglomerates have become overly powerful, due in part to the draw of celebrity culture, and they modify and transmit only the information they want the public to see and hear.

Neema clearly pointed out the media's relationship with consumer behaviour. She asked, how does social media influence consumer buying decisions? My research efforts helped me understand that targeted media can influence people to act in very specific ways that are positive for specific businesses, and social media works well with all demographics when specifically targeted at them. Social media affects consumer behavior, and influences shopping behavior, in all age groups. Most business owners and marketers have heard the refrain that social media is important. This this is certainly true; business owners can't *make* customers use social media, but they can influence what their outreach social media connects to, including shopper finds. This is why it's important to establish a social media presence and why many businesses use celebrities to advertise their products.

One thing Neema was clear about was that disseminating information can be seen as either manipulation or education, and in the end it is the responsibility of the companies who are using social media for outreach to educate and not manipulate. The role of the media should be to contribute to social change and play a central role in informing the public about what happens in the world. The media has a huge impact in the construction of public beliefs and attitudes and their relationship to social change.

In Neema's dissertation, *Media in the Celebrity Culture Sphere*, Neema shows the relationship between negative media coverage of Kerry Katona, and a hardening of attitude toward her.

Neema left behind so many admirable works. Her writing is her legacy and I hope her words will contribute to the world. I just have to look around to see the importance of the work she did, and of the pieces I selected. I can't believe my good fortune, that my daughter left me and my family such treasure. She wrote with courage and no fear of judgement. My Neema had a powerful personality for a young person of only 22 years old. It gave her writing its strength.

One of Neema's happiest times in life was when she was doing her first degree at the university in England. She had grown up to be a beautiful young woman and she was enjoying everything around her, including her studies. She was developing her writing skills and it was at this time in her life that she wrote the selected essays. Every essay is concise and well-crafted, and will appeal to most audiences. She took what she knew about her chosen topics and carefully sketched out brief outlines before completing each piece. I believe that she was telling herself, "Remember Neema, moderation is the key."

Neema was thorough in her approach. She consistently asked 'who, what, where, when and why' and made sure those questions were answered within her essays with clarity and authority. She selected topics to write about that suited her style, and she carefully fleshed out the characters she was writing about. The big picture of her writing shows that she loved what she was doing and enjoyed everything about writing. One of the essays in this collection, *A Passionate Woman*, indicates that no day passed without her saying, "I love what I am doing."

As someone who was studying broadcasting and communications, she was acutely aware of some of the hidden forces operating on social media, including 'confirmation bias'. Confirmation bias is powerful when it comes to controversial topics, such as politics. If you're like most people, the majority of your friends and followers on social media probably share your outlook, which means that the vast majority of tweets, Facebook posts, pins or other content you read on sites you like tend to express the same point of view as your own. It's natural for people to surround themselves with others of like mind, both online and offline.

On social media sites, confirmation bias can create the illusion that everybody thinks the same way, which can further create political implications. Neema was the kind of person who tried to avoid political discussion on social media. She said, "I always try to avoid anything that is likely to get into a political discussion of some sort." Neema was also careful not to put anything in her essays unless she knew it was truthful. She explored the challenge of sharing information in the modern world, and examined how it is the greatest challenge of our time, in the modern world. She had vibrant ideas which are still as vibrant in our contemporary society as when the essays were written. I can't help viewing the writings collected in *Media in the Celebrity Culture Sphere and Other Essays* with admiration.

Neema believed the media filters and shapes reality into something more titillating to its viewers. I believe media temporarily focuses on certain issues, granting them a level of importance that's automatically received by audiences. This has given the media success in shaping and molding people's perception of what to think. According to Neema's essays, this misinformation isn't just about what type of news is disseminated, but also the talent of who is reporting on the subject. On Google search I learned a lot about news and the importance of the angle of reporting in the reporting process. News angle implies the particular element, interest or determining factor that should give importance to a news story. For example, when there is a car accident, a reporter may report merely on the factual aspects, such as numbers and severity of injuries, on he or she may take the angle of human interest, such as the lives and families of the person (or people) who were killed.

There are many lessons I learned from Neema's essays. For example I learned about 'modelling of mass communication by injecting factors'. Injecting certain messages into news reporting creates specific responses in the audience. This is based on direct flow of information from sender to receiver. Yes, it is an interesting part of the process and it affects mostly passive, uneducated viewers.

Higher, educated classes of people are not as easily swayed. Education creates a knowledge gap as well as a social gap. People with education tend to have higher income, better communication skills and more knowledge than those who are poor and uneducated. They acquire information more easily and relate it to background information about their favorite topics or subjects of their choice. People of higher socio-economic status also have a more relevant social context. The nature of mass communication media is generally directed toward people of higher social-economic status.

In her essay *Media in the Culture Sphere*, Neema points toward the idea that the media is very influential and can possibly change behaviour and attitudes of the public easily. In this way, it creates mass participation. It is proof of how the power of media informs the crowd, molding perceptions and shaping realities. Social media is growing, and because of this growth, our lives are affected every single day. These effects are not all positive, but they are not all negative either. Neema's last essay looks at the audiences who follow celebrities and provides evidence of how the media and entertainment industry contribute to celebrity culture.

Businesses also use social media to influence perception as well as to improve brand loyalty. Engaging with customers via social media helps build stronger customer relationships and can set a business apart from its competition by showing audiences how the brand is different, and by reinforcing that the business cares about its customers. Consider that there are now billions of people using social networks across the globe. It is fascinating to study how businesses use social media to engage with those people. Sherpa Marketing did a study that found that more people follow *brands* on social media than follow celebrities.

People believe that if you're not using social media as a marketing tool, you're missing out on a fast, inexpensive, and effective way to reach almost half the world's population. But social media is also about saving money. Social media offers an easy, low-commitment way for customers to interact with businesses and their products. Many social networks offer advertising formats specifically designed to help people to connect, engage, and grow their business.

I decided to highlight a number of benefits. First, social media offers the opportunity to increase brand awareness (brand building). Nearly half the world's population uses social media platforms, so this is a good way to reach new and highly targeted potential customers. People don't only connect with brands they already know on social media; they use social media platforms to discover new products, and in this way it can help people connect, engage, and grow their businesses. Businesses benefit from social media because it humanizes their brands, and gives them the opportunity to connect with customers (and potential customers) in a more meaningful way. It is quite obvious that they've got to show the human side of their brand, but I think the big question here is, how are they embracing their brand values?

The next obvious question then is, do businesses even have brand values? For example, how does business look out for the best interests of their customers and employees? And more importantly, does their product really work?

The best thing for businesses to do to promote their brand values is to create real human connection, and that is one of the key benefits of social media for businesses. Social media the perfect platform for introducing online users to people who patronize specific companies. It is a way to showcase how existing customers use and benefit from products. I have learned from Google that people call this kind of behavior 'meaningful relationship moments'. The big picture of this relationship is that a social media advocacy program can be a great way to humanize your brand.

Another benefit of social media is that it can offer businesses the opportunity to establish their brand as the 'go-to' source for information on niche topics. Brand advocacy is a great way to build consumer trust and leadership. For example, LinkedIn—and in particular the LinkedIn Publishing Platform—is a great social network to use when aiming to establish yourself as a leader in a particular area. LinkedIn provides a unique approach to self-marketing.

Self-marketing is another benefit of social media. Users log into their social media accounts at least once per day, and many people also check social multiple times per day. Social media gives people the opportunity to connect with fans and followers every time they log in. If you are marketing yourself this way, keep your posts entertaining and informative, and your followers will be glad to see your new content in their feeds. They will keep you 'top of mind' so you're their first stop when they're ready to make a purchase. Social media facilitates growth by increasing website traffic. As we all know, social media posts and ads are key to driving traffic to your website.

Sharing content from a blog or website to social channels is another great way to get readers as soon as you publish a new post. Participating in social chats, and just doing what they call 'the weekly' on Twitter and other social media (including Facebook) can be a great way to increase visibility and get attention from new people. It's an opportunity to showcase your expertise and drive traffic to your website. Social media also offers an easy and low-commitment way to generate leads for potential customers to express interest in your business and your products. Lead generation is such an important benefit for business that many social networks offer advertising formats specifically designed to collect leads. For example, Renault Europe used Facebook ads that allowed people interested in learning more about a new model to book a test drive directly from Facebook with just a couple of taps, which boosted sales.

No matter what you sell, social media can help you sell it. Your social accounts are a critical part of your sales funnel—the process through which a new contact becomes a customer. As the number of people using social media continues to grow, and social sales tools evolve, social networks will become increasingly important for product search and ecommerce. When the time is right, you should align your social marketing and sales goals.

For individual sales professionals, social selling is already a critical tool. Another good strategy is to partner with influencers; word of mouth drives 20 to 50 percent of purchasing decisions. People who have a large following on social media can draw attention and followers to your brand. Research from Nielsen, Carat, and YouTube shows that collaborating with an influencer can give your brand four times more lift in brand familiarity than collaborating with a celebrity. When you get people talking about your product or company on social media, you build brand awareness and credibility, and set yourself up for more sales.

I have learned from Google that for the past couple of years, influencers have played a major role in promoting brands both locally and internationally. Interestingly, some marketing campaigns rely solely on influencers. It's normal practice, and many brands use influencers as well as celebrities. More and more businesses are taking the risk of investing in influencer marketing.

When I read this, I had two questions. First, what's the difference between celebrities and influencers? Second, how does a business choose which one it needs?

Traditional celebrities tend to be stars based on achievements in the arts. Influencers tend to only be active on social media. Both celebrities and influencers have massive social followings. Celebrities build their influence through traditional channels such as television, radio, and magazines, but they are celebrities *before* they become internet influencers. Influencers, if they are lucky, achieve fame on the internet first before expanding into traditional channels. For example, Selena

Gomez, the influencer who has the most followers on Instagram, was a celebrity first, because as a singer she gained influence through television and radio before becoming an influencer on the internet.

Promoting content on social channels is a great way to get your smart, well-researched content in front of new people, to prove your expertise and to grow your audience. For example, Adobe used LinkedIn sponsored content to showcase its research, including infographics and videos. Marketing decision-makers exposed to Adobe's promoted content were 50 percent more likely to view Adobe as shaping the future of digital marketing and 79 percent more likely to agree that Adobe could help them optimize media spending. To maximize social media for business benefits, businesses need to make sure they have a content marketing plan in place with a goal, for example, to go viral. As people start liking, commenting on, and sharing social posts, content is exposed to new audiences—their friends and followers.

Going viral takes this concept one step further; as people share your content with their networks, and their networks follow suit, your content spreads across the internet, getting thousands or even millions of shares. All those shares, likes, and comments show an existing connection with your brand. For example, if I see that my friend likes your article, I may be inclined to check out what you have to say, even if I've never heard of your company before. In a world where there is far more content than any one person could ever consume, a friend's social share acts as a kind of pre-screening.

Going viral is no easy task, but with a proper marketing strategy, it can be achieved.

There are two ways businesses can source content on social media, and the number one way to source ideas is to ask your followers what they want, or to engage in 'social listening'. Simply put, give people what they're asking for. It's a sure way to create content that people will want to read and share. The second way is to create a contest or use a hashtag to source user-generated content (UGC) you can share. This works perfectly, because getting your followers involved can build excitement about your brand while also providing you with a library of social posts to share over time. It can be a little bit overexciting, because just how much content can you get through a UGC campaign? Check out the #hashtag from various websites to see which has generated more than a certain number of posts.

There are benefits of social media for communication, including reputation management, and getting your customers talking about you, whether or not you're there to respond. If you and your team are on the ball, you can pick up on important social posts about your brand to highlight the positive and address the negative before it turns into a major issue. For example, is someone saying something about your business that's not true? If so, work out and share your side of the story in a polite, professional way. Or is someone singing your praises? Send them plenty of thanks and draw attention to their kind words.

You also get the advantage of addressing crisis situations in a timely manner that could detract from your business. If something negative has gone viral very fast, and people are talking about it, you are afforded an immediate opportunity to make it right and apologize. After this first apology, your company will know what to do next. For example, the company may follow up with several more statements on social media, and announce that it will increase the budget for staff training so the mistake doesn't recur.

It might remain to be seen what long-term effects a given incident will have, but consequences are worse if a company doesn't respond quickly and appropriately on social media. Most companies have a plan in place for dealing with a crisis, though smaller brands may not have a crisis blow up to as large a scale as larger companies. For smaller companies, a crisis can have a devastating impact within a tight-knit community or niche. Silence is not an option when it comes to responding to crises on social media. Maintaining well-run and managed social accounts and having a plan in place can help make sure a company is present and ready to engage if the worst occurs.

Social networks give businesses the opportunity to interact directly with customers and fans, and likewise they give customers the chance to interact directly with your brand. Unlike traditional media, which offers only one-way communication, social media is a two-way street. If you want customers and followers to be engaged, you have to be engaged yourself. Stay active and respond to comments and questions on your own social media posts in a way that's appropriate to your brand. Interestingly, you can also use social media monitoring to keep an eye on what people are saying across the social web.

Across the globe, employee engagement is abysmally low, including in the business sector. Why is that? Is it the company's fault or the employees' fault? Acknowledging this helps recognize that engagement is a two-way street. The company has to make an effort, but so do the employees. Employees should get engaged, instead of waiting on the company to do it for them.

Much has been written on how companies can make their work environments more engaging, and what employees can do to embrace the opportunities that may offer. They may feel better about their work by grabbing each and one of those opportunities and saying to themselves, "We can't just sit back and wait." Employees need to have some control of their work environments, and they also need to have a sense of belonging. Employees need to ask what is expected of them so they can make sure they know how to react in any given situation. They also need to be proactive and request what they need as well as be their own best advocates. They need to request the tools they really need to be effective.

Of course, there are challenges in this process, but what can you do? Brainstorm and ask questions. Can you articulate how you will go the extra mile? Can you identify a way of developing? The question indicates a business mindset which will make for better communication and, in the process, may help employees get what they are after. By asking these questions, they connect to something new, and get to know their own strengths. Then, self-realization will take them to the point where they are be able to say, "I have the opportunity to do what I do best every day." This is the starting point for knowing yourself, knowing what you are uniquely good at, and knowing what you do best.

The ability to figure out what is fundamentally important to an organization or company is a win-win situation for both employer and employee. The company gets the very best from the employee, and the employee is fulfilled and is feels like he or she is making a real contribution. To influence the type of attention you get and recognition you receive brings attention in a positive way, so people know the contributions you've made.

Every employee contributes something a little different to the organization or company, though they generally have very little influence over the mission or purpose of the organization. But every company practices something different in its working culture, and the culture is what helps employees stay on the right track. For the company to exist it's important to think outside the box and to work well with others.

Who are those 'others'? How does your company affect their lives? Asking these questions helps identify what you can do for them. It's important to be explicit about the connection between your work and the individual lives that are affected. This puts value on the work and gives meaning to it. If you can't make a connection with your company's purpose, what about your department or division? How can being great at your work have an effect on someone else's happiness, productivity, or stress level? Virtually every job can have a meaningful effect on someone else. Embracing this will make your job inherently more satisfying and produce better teamwork.

Don't be afraid to get help and support, and invest your time in finding a mentor. And if you are in the position of being a mentor, remember one of the most rewarding things people can do in life is help others. Being kind is something you should do anyway, but it can also help you achieve your goals.

Some people enjoy collaboration more than others. It certainly comes with complications, but it can be very beneficial. While it is hard to directly influence higher echelon associates in a larger company, pay attention to what teams, departments, and divisions have the greatest success. Be conscious of those groups and look for opportunities to work with them. If that's not possible, do your best to look for opportunities to imitate what they are doing. Discuss with your associates what makes those groups successful and what it might look like if your own group operated that way. People will start thinking of you as a team player, and they'll appreciate your desire for improvement.

One of the best ways to connect and engage in your job is to make close friends. Cultivating friends at work is important because it creates strong teams. Friendships require investment, and all of us can take time to ask someone to lunch or to happy hour. Find out about their interests, families, passions and goals, and see if they fit with your interests. These connections will make your day-to-day life more pleasant. More important, this will make your own work more meaningful and make the work environment more engaging and enjoyable. Strong relationships at work can even help make personal relationships at home better.

Another way to engage at work is to solicit feedback. Never underestimate the power of feedback, and seek it regularly. Every employee should be able to say what they have accomplished, for example, in the last six months. The big question here is, what if your employees haven't accomplished anything? You should initiate this at least every six months to ensure steady forward progression in your company. You don't need formal performance reviews—what you need is a sense of direction. Employees should ask themselves: Am I adding value? Is the work aligning with what was expected? Is my progression aligning with what is normal? What is on the horizon?

These questions are critical to an employee's continuous growth and it also demonstrates how hard a person is willing to work to make him- or herself and the company better. Employees reflect on their experience and take stock of their own progress. For example, an employee can say, "In this last year, have I had opportunities at work to learn and grow," and the employer should want to help their employees to achieve their goals.

Research has shown that a critical ingredient in learning and growth is the process of reflection. Think back on all the projects you've completed, the conversations you've had, and the decisions you've made. What skills did you enhance? Have you become a more thoughtful employee?

In the publication, *Learning and Leading with Habits of Mind* by Arthur L. Costa and Bena Kallick, Chapter 12 is called, *Learning Through Reflection*. The authors state, "Reflection has many facets. For example, reflecting on work enhances its meaning. Reflecting on experiences encourages insight and complex learning. We foster our own growth when we control our learning, so some reflection is best done alone. Reflection is also enhanced, however, when we ponder our learning with others."

Social media can be used as a reflective tool as well as a way to promote business and market products. It is a way to solicit feedback and actively engage with an audience. Social media advises about the benefit of the service the company is providing, including customer service and support. Research published in the *Harvard Business Review* (HBR) shows that brands that don't meet those expectations damage their bottom line. The HBR research, which specifically looks at Tweets, shows that customers who receive a response to their Tweet would be willing to spend more on the brand on a later purchase, especially if they get a response within five minutes. That holds true even when their initial Tweet was a flat-out complaint.

Monitoring conversations that are relevant to your brand is another crucial component. Monitoring is an important element of audience engagement. It's the key source of intelligence about your brand, your competitors, and your niche. Social media contributes to helping business to learn more about their customers. Social media generates a huge amount of data about customers in real time. Businesses can use that information to make smarter business decisions.

All major social networks offer analytics that provide demographic information about the people interacting with your account. This can help you tailor your business and marketing strategy to better speak to your real audience. Facebook, Instagram, Twitter, LinkedIn, Snapchat, and Pinterest have extensive guides on how to use analytics so there's no excuse to remain in the dark about your customers and social followers.

Gauging sentiment around branding is another benefit of social media. Lots of 'mentions' are a good thing, in most cases. But if you're getting lots of mentions with a negative sentiment, you need to do some quick thinking to figure out what's gone wrong and address the problem. While it's important to know how much people are talking about your brand online, it's also important to know how people actually feel about your brand. Social media allows you to stay on top of sentiment analysis so you can protect your brand reputation.

You can get step-by-step social media strategy guides with pro tips on how to grow your social media presence. It is more than beneficial to keep an eye on the competition. It's also important to know what people are saying about your competitors. For example, tracking mentions of your competitors might reveal pain points with their products that you could address, winning new customers in the process.

Consider when Uber Canada launched a promotion to deliver free ice cream for a day in Vancouver. Things went spectacularly wrong. People couldn't get their free ice cream, and they were not happy about it. They took to social media to complain.

Monitoring the competition on social media means you'll be aware when your competitors launch new products, run promotions, and release new reports or data. Winning and staying on top of industry news is important. In the online world, things move fast—and you can't afford to be left behind. Keeping a virtual ear to the ground through social listening makes sure you're always informed about upcoming changes to your industry that could affect the way you do business.

Social media includes targeted advertising. Social ads are an inexpensive way to promote your business and distribute content. They also offer powerful targeting options so you can reach the right audience and make the most of your budget. Savvy marketers have embraced this key benefit of social media for business. They spent twice as much on Facebook ads in 2018 as they did on newspaper advertising. With ads targeting options including demographic information, geography, language, and even online behaviors, businesses can craft specific messages that best speak to different groups of potential customers, and only pay for the exact viewers they want to reach.

A Google search reveals that nearly 70 percent of online shopping carts are abandoned. People who abandon products in a shopping cart are potential customers. They have already found your website, browsed your products, and made a decision about what they might want. People abandon shopping carts for many reasons, but someone who has expressed this degree of interest in your company should not be ignored Therefore, by using tracking tools like Facebook Pixel, you can show these potential customers social media ads for the exact products they have browsed on your website or placed in the shopping cart.

Reporting and analytics are useful tools for providing return on investment (ROI). With social media tracking and analytics tools, you can see the full impact of your social media activities, from followers to engagements, right through to purchases.

Neema worked with the BBC and other media companies in the United Kingdom as well as agencies around the world and her essays discuss information dissemination, with an emphasis on accessibility and diversity, including the creation, shaping and exchange of ideas provided by the media platform. Neema's work builds a greater understanding of how media impacts people's day to day lives. For me as her mother, her essays also show how she worked extremely hard to achieve her academic goals. She stayed focused and made sure she did exactly what she was asked to do, and that she understood why she was being asked to do it. The broader theme in her work was always, what's the wider context for media interest? But the broader theme from a personal perspective was that Neema was passionate and loved what she was doing. She would have had an amazing career in broadcasting if she had lived. She would have contributed to understanding in the world, because of how she was.

Neema paid attention to ethically sensitive issues. Sometimes, when I read her work, I feel I can hear her asking such things as, "Neema, could your findings be mispresented? What would be the implications of that? Have you made some mistakes? What steps do you need to take to ensure that won't happen?" In *Media in the Celebrity Culture Sphere*, she touches on some controversial issues, including online bullying, for example. And in *Essay Number Six,* Neema she highlights a few questions about highly sensitive issues that might lead to thought-provoking debates and make the audience ponder.

The essays have one strong message—that social media has become a significant source of information for many individuals and that the information industry regards social media as the best way of spreading information in a timely manner. But so many things can go wrong. False information can spread rapidly, creating negative social impact and even serious economic loses.

Other things she brings up include the importance of editorial insight and technical review, as well as time management appropriate training. In an industry that influences so many people, there is no room for error.

CHAPTER 5

Essay #1: Cornwall Film Festival

*M*aking my way out of screen hall four on the first night of the Cornwall Film Festival, I found myself wondering where everyone was. It felt like a small-time event, yet I was pretty sure that was not going to be the case.

Outside the hall on the upper floor of the Phoenix Cinema in Falmouth, I realised that it was indeed *not* a small-time event. Groups of people were out and about, standing, moving around and seated at fancy tables. They were chatting away with friends and acquaintances or introducing themselves to random strangers while sampling the variety of delicacies making their way around.

We had just come from watching the first feature of the night, a series of short, high concept dance films by South East Dance. I'm a keen dancer and was especially looking forward to this feature. I wasn't sure what to expect when I turned up to see this feature, but I came out utterly impressed. It was beautifully choreographed and shot, enticing and energetic; I found myself making a mental note to dance a little when I got home.

Next was the sunny and light-hearted *Marcello, Marcello*. Admittedly, before reading a synopsis of the story, and even before looking at the colourful books placed out for display and purchase at the entrance to the cinema, I wrongly assumed that I was going to be served with a biopic about an aging opera singer's life. It turned out to be the complete opposite of this. It was fresh and engaging. It was a very colourful romantic comedy, whose main themes of tradition and cultural values were cleverly depicted by very talented actors; a beautiful 'coming of age' story, told in very unfamiliar surroundings, yet very easy for anyone to engage with.

Perhaps the most captivating, if not thrilling, film for me was *The Girl With The Dragon Tattoo* that came next. The slow and dragging start aside, this ultimate feminist fantasy provided a much-needed, mind stimulating experience with its witty dialogue, hard action and a female main character who was so complex that at first that I was not sure if I was supposed to be looking at her as the underdog, the victim of fate, or just simply a scheming rebellious spirit. I was especially impressed by the fact that even the sexual scenes that seemed over the top were tastefully done.

The first day of the festival ended on a high and I couldn't wait for Saturday and all that it had to offer.

Saturday, for me, started off with a very well written Cornish feature, *Bad Company*. This classic tale of obsession was delivered with immaculate performances from the actors. It gave an insight into the kind of production that is possible with a small budget film, especially for independent student film makers. The Q&A session with the producer afterwards was very useful and educational.

The other Cornish feature was *The Diary Of A Disgraced Soldier.* Although I wasn't keen on watching this feature in the first place, mainly because I always try to avoid anything that is likely to get into a political discussion of some sort, I found it very thought-provoking. It gave me a glimpse of how life can be for those directly affected by war. It was a tale of a soldier wanting to be heard, and seeking closure. The support from the local people who turned out to see this feature and participate in the Q&A session was really overwhelming. It demonstrated how important a sense of community is to them was and how especially aware they were of the political situation in the country, in relation to the war in Iraq. This was very refreshing.

The last feature for me was the much-hyped *The Men Who Stare At Goats.* I left this film thinking (after I had read that it was based on a true story), 'Did this really happen? That's ridiculous.' The whole concept was absurd (all the more reason to love it) and I kicked myself for not attending the lectures on campus from the writer, Jon Ronson. Now I had to rely on the internet to find out more about the story behind it, which was less impressive than being in the physical presence of the person responsible for creating it. I wasn't sure about the casting of George Clooney in this film, but his performance was spectacular.

Overall, for me as a first timer, the festival was a wonderful and eye-opening experience.

Reflection:

In this essay, Neema wrote about viewing different films at the Cornwall Film Festival, including one about dance. She wrote that the beauty of dancing, and the traditional and cultural values of dancing, were important to her. Dancing for pleasure, or to entertain others, has been done by people from all backgrounds for centuries. The challenging question is, what is the biggest benefit of social dance? My research indicates that dancing has a number of benefits including as a way to engage others at social gatherings and for exercise.

Dancing is a series of rhythmic and patterned bodily movements, usually performed to music. Dance movements have a wide range of physical and mental benefits and can improve:

- condition of heart and lungs
- muscular strength
- endurance and motor fitness
- aerobic fitness
- muscle tone and strength
- weight management
- bone strength, and
- coordination.

Neema wrote that dancing is good for the body and said, "I came out utterly impressed … I found myself making a mental note to dance a little when I got home." I believe Neema went home and danced that day.

She also wrote about her impression of the most captivating, thrilling film, *The Girl With Dragon Tattoo.* I saw the film as well as read the book and I believe the author, Stieg Larsson, would agree with what Neema wrote about this film. She provides a short analysis and examines the film in her insightful way.

The Girl With the Dragon Tattoo, was a #1 New York Times Bestseller. The 2011 film was based on the novel by Stieg Larsson, and the American version starred Rooney Mara as Lisbeth and Daniel Craig as journalist Mikael Blomkvist. It put Rooney Mara on the map and earned her a Best Actress Oscar nomination and A-list status.

While the heart of the story appealed to audiences across the globe, behind the scenes, the fight to get the franchise to American audiences was one of great turmoil. From an intense casting process, to a seven year wait for a sequel, the backstory of this franchise may be even more interesting than the gritty noir movie itself. The first book was published after Stieg Larsson's death, and according to a Google search, the author originally planned on writing ten books for this series, which he called The Millennium series. Unfortunately, he passed away suddenly in 2004. The Swedish title was *Män som hatar kvinnor,* which translates in English to Men Who Hate Women.

In all, three of Larsson's books were published. A fourth book will probably never see the light of day because while Larsson's father and brother may have been happy to continue the series, Larsson's girlfriend of 30 years, Eva Gabrielsson, had a very different opinion. The couple never married, which unfortunately meant Gabrielsson had no rights when it came to the work and estate of her late lover, but it is believed that she is in possession of Larsson's laptop, which has the beginning of what would have been the fourth book in the series. But if Gabrielsson has anything to say about it, there is zero likelihood she will ever release it.

Personally, I'm disappointed because I think about Stieg Larsson's in the same way I think about Neema's. He meant to share his thoughts and creativity with the world and I think he should be honored in this way.

However, I am doing this for Neema because there is something unique about mother and daughter relationships. Neema and I were best friends, and we had similar interests. It was fun to be together and, more important to me, we always had something to talk about. We had our own unique hobbies and interests, but we looked at things the same way. I am certain that she would want her valuable work to be read by others.

CHAPTER 6

Essay #2: TV Review— A Passionate Woman, Episode 2 (Final)

*I*t's the 80s and Betty is now middle-aged, with a handsome son who is about to get married to his Australian girlfriend. In Episode 1, we saw Betty's mother in some kind of hospice/home. Well, you see her mental state wasn't all there, or as Donald (Betty's husband) put it, "You have to admit, she's a bit crackers."

Well, it looks like Betty went a bit crackers, too, when her son revealed he was planning to move to Australia. He was all she had. She gave all her love to him after that Craze affair and neglected not only herself, but also her husband. There is a lesson here: There is only so much you can invest in other people, what about yourself? What happens when these people are gone? Anyway, she decides to tell her son (Mark) about that affair and how she has never got over it, or over Craze's murder. She goes even further to tell him that she never really loved Donald. I don't know about you, but I'd never tell my children I never loved their father. Such things you keep them to yourself, but there you go.

It was not all doom and gloom, actually. Things got more unbearable, but with that came closure. Betty found Moira (Craze's wife) and blurted out about the affair. Moira went ballistic but actually assured Betty that in no way was she special. Craze was a philanderer and there were more women just like her who thought they were made of some stuff, and that Craze loved them, oh so much. You can imagine how Betty took this. The bastard duped her! She later walks out of her son's wedding and gets herself on top of a roof with the intent of committing suicide, but her Donald comes to rescue her and they have the most intense conversation of their lives. Donald tells her how much he loves her, now more so.

She realizes that's what love is about. Sticking in there and loving someone even when they don't want you, and being there for them and providing for them, which I also agree with. Not that passionate open-your-legs-right now business she had going on with Craze. She realizes that she actually did love Donald (obviously honey, otherwise you wouldn't have stayed with him that long) and off they go into the air. Yes, Donald booked an air balloon for them after the wedding reception, partly for her and partly for himself: They were going to be flying to Australia frequently to visit their son and he needed to practice, so he said.

Overall, it was a happy ending, which we all love. I know I do, and Donald cried (you know he never does this mushy stuff). How sweet. A very good series, although Episode 2 could have done without the clichés (we know you are meant to be a passionate woman, Betty, there is no need to spell it out) and the flashbacks (although most of them had the handsome Craze in them, so I'm not complaining much).

Reflection:

The review of *A Passionate Woman* that Neema wrote raises some fundamental questions about relationships immediately. Neema immersed herself in, and wrote about, the meaning, and advantages and disadvantages, of investing our time in other people. Relationships are something we all experience in our lives, so she touched on a universal theme. She wrote because she wanted to tell people that it's important not to forget about ourselves when we are busy caring for others. This is the bigger question Neema brought to the reader's attention. She wrote, "… there is only so much you can invest in other people, what about yourself? What happens when these people are gone?"

Neema was talking about the real-life experiences we have in our lives, and telling us that when we invest hopes and emotions in other people, which is a normal thing to do, sometimes we can shortchange ourselves. Good relationships protect our mental health and wellbeing and it has been proven that those who are socially connected are happier, physically healthier and live longer lives. However, it is important to protect yourself and nurture yourself as well. These people may leave you someday.

Romantic relationships, romantic partnership and marriage (which is what Neema is discussing in her essay) are built upon affection, trust, intimacy, and romantic love. We usually experience this kind of relationship with only one person at a time. But there are other kinds of relationships too, such as friendships and other kinds of partnerships. Neema advocated for a good balance when investing in people. She implies that investment can help a relationship, as it elicits positive feelings that have benefits later on.

From a monetary point of view, for example when people merge finances because they've married or moved in together, relationships can have benefits. However, you should never put the monetary side before the investment of love and care. Ideally, a relationship balances both.

Powerful boosts in a relationship can be made when a couple feel grateful for, and committed to, one another. Neema wrote about her concern when people invest too much in relationships and how they feel when they have done so and the person leaves or dies. She talks about the importance of investing in others, as people tend to invest a great deal in others, especially in romantic relationships. We put time, energy, and emotions into our relationships and we tie up our material possessions in them too. We make sacrifices for our partners, both small and large, but make less investment in ourselves. This is what she meant when she mentioned the relationship 'you have with yourself'. Self-care is about looking after yourself and your mental health.

From a business point of view, investing in people is when you work to create a long-term, sustainable business that features a friendly and inviting working environment and a place people feel privileged to work at and contribute to every day. Why should you invest in people? When you invest, you put time or money into something and hope there will be returns greater than what was originally put in. This is a powerful statement—invest in people, and they will invest in you.

I try to maintain this approach with the Neema Foundation. For example, I try to listen to our team and reward them in different and unique ways. I feel it is mandatory to affirm them and their work. I have experienced positive affirmation myself. When I share my knowledge publicly, I enjoy the interest from the audience and the applause and questions. That's because it's good to have external affirmation. One thing I know from my life experience is that we all are human beings. We are not perfect, but are all learning day by day. Mistakes are educational bonding opportunities. If you hire qualified people who are passionate about their work, and create a special team and environment that people want to be a part of, mistakes are opportunities for growth. I tell people that we must have a unified vision and goal and work to help each individual learn, grow and reach their maximum potential.

Investing in your people is one of the best productivity strategies. Working outside the box and finding meaning in what you are doing creates a good corporate culture. Nurturing your employees creates a positive cycle, because when you build their confidence and give them tools to learn skills for the next evolution of your business (and their careers), over time, it feeds back into the organization.

What does it mean to 'invest in you'? Investing in yourself means you stop drifting through life waiting for things to happen, and instead take concrete actions that bring you closer to your best self. It is banking on yourself; one of the best returns on investments you can have. Whether it's investing in learning a new skill, developing yourself personally or professionally, tapping into your creativity or hiring a coach, you need to give to yourself first before you can give to others. It is our responsibility to take the time to develop our gifts and talents, so we can best serve others. Investing in yourself is an example of self-love; you must love yourself before you can expect others to love you.

Neema wrote about the importance of being proactive in the workplace and suggested it was a good idea to do a better job of advocating for you, and only you. For example, you can make your case to the human resources department that you need a pay raise, rather than just accept a standard percentage increase based on a number that is too low. The message here is that when you love yourself and invest in yourself as an individual, you prove to the world (including your workplace) that you have value.

We all have unique experiences that shape us. It is good when something you feel inside you tells you the impact is real. This feeds into how you encourage and teach others to see their value and abilities. Therefore, increasing the ability to negotiate and create safe spaces for open conversations about all issues affecting people at a workplace is desirable. Being able to discuss things like salary and benefits can increase morale and motivate individuals to become more productive. Investing in *you* is as important as investing in other people and it means putting resources into relationships, appreciating relationships and being willing to stay in relationships. It is also important that you commit yourself to help this relationship grow in the future—including the relationship with yourself.

The relationship you have with yourself is crucial to your own wellbeing, as is creating healthy and happy relationships with others. Being kind to yourself is one of the best things you can do for yourself. Loneliness can be toxic to our wellbeing—our health declines earlier and we have shorter lifespans. It's good to have supportive relationships to protect our bodies and our minds. Investing in yourself is powerful, because it sends a powerful message to yourself and the world that you possess value and potential, and that you will give it the energy, space and time to grow and create results. Investing in yourself emotionally, physically, spiritually and financially will allow you to become the best version of yourself. When you are the best version of yourself, you will be able to handle situations when other people are gone.

My research journey helped me to understand better about different ways to invest in yourself. The first and most important thing is to set personal and business goals. If you're not taking the time to set goals, it's like driving in the dark with the headlights turned off. You will not know where you're going and you will waste precious time. For example former Federal Reserve Chairman Ben Bernanke shared his perspective in 2007 when he said, "When I travel around the country, meeting with students, businesspeople, and others interested in the economy, I am occasionally asked for investment advice ... I know the answer to the question and I will share it with you today: Education is the best investment'.

Second, take time to honor your intuition. You can show yourself love by trusting your gut and honoring the message that it's sending. Listening to your intuition will allow you to make better decisions. Valuing your intuition, by not allowing the thoughts, feelings or statements of others to take away from what you know to be true, is very empowering. Paying attention to how you feel will help you make better, smarter and quicker decisions.

Third, invest time in your creativity, no matter what your age. Creativity doesn't diminish as we get older. Some people believe the peak of creativity in is around 30 to 40 years old, but creativity and lifelong learning are available to us all. Creativity can be the catalyst in the manifestation of continual learning and lifelong activity. People can be inspired, have fun and appreciate the beauty in the world at any age.

The big question here is, how does one invest in their creativity? Considering that the world is changing very fast, and technology is evolving so quickly that competitive advantages based on it are short-lived, it's good to stay focused. The most valuable and sustainable competitive advantage is one's ability to innovate relentlessly and adapt in the face of change. We all have made countless investments in ourselves over the years, both good and bad. Sometimes different perspectives involve similar approaches, which can cause struggle.

Studies have demonstrated that working with limited resources can force us to be more creative. Then you can see clearly your ability to face challenges and be open to talk about them. Challenges are good because they create novel results. People even artificially create challenges and constraints in order to bolster their creative abilities and become better problem-solvers.

Personally, when I have a certain project which requires me to meet a tight budget or deadline, I ensure I have the skills to get the job done efficiently. When I get more than I initially planned for, such as a bigger budget or more resources, I am grateful to be in position of creating far more value.

Learning a new language is helpful for becoming more creative. Evidence suggests that bilingualism can improve the brain's executive function, which we use for planning, problem solving, staying focused, and many other activities that are critical to professional success. As a native Swahili speaker, learning English was a necessary investment for my career in business. But the greater benefit of learning this second language was how it shaped my new way of thinking. Learning a new language made my brain more malleable, and I began to spot patterns and problems that I wouldn't have otherwise. Anyone learning a new language usually also spends time with, and learns from, people of different backgrounds, which is perhaps the greatest benefit of all. When you travel, you connect with other cultures in a profound way and it is possible you learn their languages as well.

Expanding your expertise is another way to develop creativity. Many people believe you should master a single skill and become the best at it, rather than trying to be good at multiple things, and to an extent, I agree. However, the benefit of mastering more than one thing is that you have more choices in life and are more flexible. The whole picture comes together more rapidly when you master two worlds, for example research and finances. You can bring them together in a way that will introduce hot ideas to into your workplace and create a competitive advantage.

This has held true for me. Becoming adept at managing finances and applying social research is what enabled me to create the Neema Edward Mkwelele Wellness Foundation. I acquired knowledge in two distinct areas, and was able to connect the dots to find new ways to solve problems in ways others may not have considered.

Another creative strategy for me was to learn computer programming. These days, every industry is a technology industry. Learning computer programming has similar benefits to learning a new language. When you learn to code, you boost your problem-solving skills, because you learn how to think differently. Learning to code trains you to think in a certain way. It teaches you to ask the right questions, accurately evaluate your opportunities and review risks, think creatively, and more.

My understanding of coding and technology in general has informed my approach to data analysis. Interestingly, this ties back to previous comments I made about the idea that there is a lot to gain from investing in yourself. To excel at not just one, but two different areas is desirable.

While hard skills like financial management and computer programming are paramount in the modern world, you might be surprised to find that the majority of employers actually rate 'soft skills', such as good communication abilities, higher. Whether your charge is inspiring your employees as a leader, sharing status updates as a project manager, or detailing the technical requirements for a new software build, the ability to communicate clearly is universally vital. This is why public speaking classes are such a rewarding way to invest in yourself. No matter how good you think you may be at communicating, public speaking classes will push you to get even better. They open a controlled environment for the kind of constructive criticism that you've likely never heard from any boss or employee. Public speaking classes helped me learn to articulate my thoughts and ideas more precisely, build deeper emotional connections with my audience, and gain a new sense of confidence. These skills have in turn enriched both my personal and professional lives. Public speaking classes are also useful for become more creative which is rewarding in today's competitive workforce.

Investing in yourself is a great way for building your confidence. People who know their own value have something to say, and others listen. Neema asked, why is it so important to invest in yourself? The answer is that you develop an understanding of your own value what you can offer others. It's very important for every individual to understand their own worth because it gives courage to speak your own truth. The more you love yourself and own the value that you offer, the more confident you will become in sharing it with others. This includes taking care of your health. Eat right each day, and fuel your body with nutrients. When you focus on eating organic food and make healthier choices, you will feel better and have more energy. Work on avoiding instant gratification and eating unhealthy food. If you're like me, you'll regret it later. Exercise daily, and do something every day to get your heart rate up, even if it's just walking the dog. Exercise gives you the energy to take on the day with confidence, because of how it makes you feel.

Investing in yourself also extends to educating yourself. Books and audiobooks are an awesome way to build knowledge and expertise in any area. Attending seminars and workshops expands your knowledge and skills in both your business and personal life. It also gives you the opportunity to meet and interact with like-minded individuals.

Finally, the last thing to do is to choose to be happy. Research indicates that happiness is a choice. Happy people choose to focus on the positive aspects of life rather than the negative. They are not held hostage by their circumstances. They look at all the reasons to be grateful. Simply try, and you will be surprised that a little effort can go a long way to increasing happiness. Make happiness your number one goal, because happy people live longer, healthier lives. This point clarifies the importance of investing in you. Learn good self-management skills, good interpersonal skills, and good career-related skills. Choose to be in environments and around people who increase your probability of happiness. The people who become the happiest, and grow the most, are those who make their own personal growth a priority. Linger on little, positive moments—this is another way of experiencing happiness.

The secret to happiness could be as simple (and difficult) as becoming more mindful. Meditation is a practice anyone can do, anywhere, as long as they're willing to sit and try to silence the mind. Is thought to be a happiness-booster. Learn to enjoy the silence and you might be surprised at the outcome.

Try smiling your way to happiness, success and motivation. Boosting your mood by smiling and don't forget to practice gratitude. Gratitude is the only way to cultivate thankfulness. Practicing gratitude is a scientifically backed way to increase happiness, and it's firmly within your control to choose to be more grateful. Grateful people tend to appreciate simple pleasures, defined as, 'those pleasures in life that are available to most people', according to a report in the *Journal of Social Behavior and Personality*. Define and pursue your own happiness, find happiness, and you will find success. Conventional thinking has it that pursuing success will lead to happiness, but research has shown that it may be just the opposite. Let yourself be happy. And, like Neema, take time to dance.

In her review of *A Passionate Woman*, Neema touched on love, although briefly. She seems to agree with one of the main characters, and she wrote, "Donald booked an air balloon for them after the wedding reception, partly for her and partly for himself; they were going to be flying to Australia to visit their son and he needed to practice that … overall, a happy ending which we all love."

What Neema was communicating was about unconditional love. Unconditional love is part of what it means to be a human being. Sometimes we take it for granted, but it is one of the basic needs for human wellbeing. In her essay, Neema offers inspiration to those who have questions, struggles or challenges and she provides an answer to the common question, is unconditional love really possible? She seems to be saying that yes, it is, but only if individuals are willing to work and make it possible. As challenging as it may be, we all want to be loved as we are—and perhaps we'd like to see ourselves as capable of selfless love. But, unfortunately, loving unconditionally may set us up for disappointment and shame when our ideal doesn't match the reality of how difficult and/or impossible it is to love unconditionally.

There have been a number of discussions about love. The age-old question is, what is unconditional love? Unconditional love is loving someone, flaws and all, just the way they are. As the name would suggest, it means loving someone without conditions. You don't love a person on the condition that they will stay young and thin for all eternity; you love them based on who they are as a person. Tough, right?

Neema wrote that the characters on the TV show she was analyzing were able to love unconditionally. The couple's situation on the show is similar to situations for all couples around the world who agree to this statement: for better or worse. Generally, mature love can only thrive under certain conditions; just as a rose needs ample sun, water, and nutrients to survive and flourish, we cannot expect love to thrive under sterile or hostile conditions. There needs to be enough mutual respect and reasons for people to keep working on it.

Part of love is honoring boundaries, while both continue to 'do the loving'. This is what Neema was talking about. Love doesn't mean always supplying what another person wants, being tirelessly accepting, and having no needs of our own. If love saddles us with the obligation to satisfy every need, soothe every sorrow, and comply with every request, nothing good happens and we wind up berating ourselves for not being spirituality evolved if we fall short of that ideal. Today's couples experience the same thing as couples throughout time, because the challenge in every healthy relationship is being responsive to our partner while also affirming our own needs and longings. This means investing in ourselves, and honoring ourselves enough to have limits and set boundaries.

Principally, loving means being sensitive to the space between us and others and focusing on being respectful, attentive, and attuned to each other's feelings and wants. It means slowing down, staying connected to our bodies, and allowing ourselves to be affected by what others feel and want. Love asks us to take another's requests seriously to make them happy, if we can do so without harming ourselves. It doesn't mean feeling obligated always to say 'yes.' But it does mean that declining a request must be done with respect and sensitivity, rather than in a harsh or dismissive way, which damages trust. Or it means working things out so that both partner's needs can be met. A key to the elusive intimacy we seek is letting ourselves be seen while seeing another's inner life. The process of sharing and being responsive to our respective inner worlds is usually more important than the outcome.

One thing I know for sure is that you must do your best and keep the fire burning, meaning love requires an expansive and spacious presence. It cannot flourish if we ignore or minimize our partner's needs. Overall, neither can it thrive if we deny our own desires, which can create resentment. Part of a loving bond is trusting that our partner is strong enough to experience occasional disappointment when we're not inclined to be accommodating and therefore, trusting that being true to ourselves won't damage the relationship, as long as we do it kindly.

Neema talked about healthy relationships between couples and implies that a healthy relationship doesn't mean fusing or merging. We're separate people who have differences that require respect. The popular view of unconditional love fails to recognize the importance of developing frustration tolerance when things don't go our way. Relationships become stronger when we both have a capacity for self-soothing as well as taking care of ourselves emotionally when soothing from others is not forthcoming.

Basically, love cannot mean that our partner must deny their desires in order to accommodate us. Nor can it mean suppressing our own longings in order to wear the spiritual badge of honor of being unconditionally loving. In this way, partnerships are equivalent to dancing with fire. Neema used the characters from *A Passionate Woman* to provide evidence of how the fire of another's burning needs, and the fire of our own desires interact, which is a central part of the art of loving.

With the confession of the main character, honesty comes to the fore. Love cannot thrive without courageous self-awareness and rigorous honesty, both with ourselves and others. Is our 'no' to a request payback for perceived injuries? If so, this brings up fundamental questions such as, are we perpetuating a power struggle? Have we stored up hurts and resentments that leak out? To a large extent, healthy relationships require knowing our feelings, limits, and motivations. Is it really too painful to visit our in-laws? Or do we want our partner to feel the pain we're carrying from some past event? The greatest gift we can give another person is the gift of our own personal growth. The more we know ourselves and develop the courage and skills to communicate our inner experience, the more trust and love can flourish.

Unconditional love doesn't mean staying with a partner no matter how poorly they treat us, or how destructive it is for us. That violates self-love, as it is being unkind to the self. But helping others, no matter how complicated your relationship with them, is unconditional love. When about the main character tries to commit suicide, her husband came to rescue her, no matter what.

Unconditional love is possible when couples are committed to the process of open, honest, nonviolent communication. They pose themselves in a way that shows they are committed to offering a sacred, spacious, non-defensive presence, and are listening as best they can and taking their beloved's feelings and wants seriously, while also expressing their own. Couples should be moved by love and caring, not duty or obligation. Effectively, love overrides little annoyances that occur in every relationship. Couples accept differences and work with them skillfully. They also share power and, as Neema talked about, they don't always get exactly what they want.

CHAPTER 7

Essay #3: Critical Reflective Document

Documentary Production

I analysed what was required for this radio documentary, and the options I had, and realised it was going to be very helpful and inspirational to look at different examples of this form of work that have been made in the past. I listened to most of the work produced by the Sound Portraits Production organisation and got a very good idea of how this type of documentary works. I came to a decision and decided to do this in two different ways. First, to carry out interviews and then second, to give my 'actors' the chance to speak for themselves without my interruption. I was, however, going to brief them in advance before the interview so that they could give the answers in a distinctive and descriptive way and in relation to the topic at hand. I would then combine these stories with their own recorded pieces.

I sought to work with at least two people (or even more) of different ages and experience (living in Cornwall) to provide a varied and unique outlook. This would ensure that listeners engaged and focused on learning new things and getting different insights into these people's lives. I was, however, going to blend it in a way that was subtle so that listeners would feel a change in viewpoints and opinions, but not be quick to realise the difference between these people.

Radio pieces that have influenced this production and have helped me get very good structural and practical ideas for my own work include most of the spectacular pieces from the sound portraits website, such as the youth portrait series which documented the lives of different youths, their views on different aspects of their communities and their personal lives. I listened to this and was captivated by the manner in which most of these documentaries appeared to be very unserious, unofficial and carefree in their form of presenting themselves to the audience, yet they deal with very important and serious issues, issues that made the listeners feel connected and get into the lives of these 'actors'. These pieces used aspects if the dialogue structure, background noise and the music, to create this effect.

After deciding, and putting down the ideas for the characters of my piece (which included evaluating aspects like age), I set out to find these particular people. It was a bit difficult to find these people and more so to persuade them to take part in this particular project. I found that most shied away from the idea of being interviewed and having to answer questions face to face.

However I found one willing person who was ready to take part in this. I was very intrigued by the fact that he was a member of a local band and I thought that aspect would bring a lot of colour to the piece, since he would get to talk a bit about the band and his life as a musician around Cornwall. It turned out that the band was very committed and busy with their schedule for an extended period of time and as a result I could not work with him, or them for that matter, as he had to be with his bandmates.

I decided to change my view a bit and offer different options to my participants. I contacted groups of people I was interested in and offered them the freedom of documenting their stories in my absence provided they stuck to the main idea and concept of the piece. I found that this yielded more results and I at least had some willing participants.

I settled for one college student who has lived in the county for twelve years and was at that stage in his life where a lot was happening for him both personally and socially in his community. I used the stereo mic and the Fostex recorder to help him record himself, although I was not entirely pleased with some of the sound quality produced. The main reason for this, I would have to conclude, was because had never used this equipment before, so maybe couldn't adjust the specific settings to an excellent level, even though I showed him how to work it and explained everything. I found that I had to do a lot of adjusting to the original recording to achieve the desired results for the final piece.

In general, I feel that most of my aims have been met in this piece. I wanted to achieve that fresh, unscripted sound to the final piece and I achieved this because I eliminated any aspect of an interviewer and interviewee, so the final piece does not feel staged and there are no awkward moments, pauses or loss of words. My aim has also been to educate and let listeners in on the issues that are affecting this young person's life, both private issues (getting a job or continuing with his studies) and issues affecting his community as well (the economy, the issue of policing in his area, youth victimisation and the job market). This helps the listener not only to understand this particular person, but also to question whether they can identify with him or her. The aim was to create debate and ask them about important issues, such as the aspect of security in Cornwall, how young people feel about their lives in the county with regard to education and opportunity, and also about his sense of pride in the county and what he loves about it.

The most important aspect of learning that I have taken from this whole experience is the idea of networking and how important it is in for spreading ideas and intentions for different projects, and getting responses from interested individuals. As much as the project was about making unique pieces of work, the whole process of getting the word out there so as to reach interested individuals who might take part in it, or share their bit of information about this topic, has been through spreading the word and virtual 'cold calling' on social media (such as MySpace and Twitter).

Of course I targeted the local audience and made sure to explain the concept of the project.

I appreciate that I have a learnt a significant number of things from this project and I would definitely want to work on a project similar to this again, although I think I would prefer it if it was bigger and had more time dedicated to it. Most importantly, I have realised how crucial it is to find the subjects for such types of projects well in advance so that they can have time to digest the concept and give it their best. It also would have helped me in preparing more detailed ideas, given me enough time to cancel the ones that were not required anymore, and work on improving the ones with more potential. Then I could present them to potential subjects in a descriptive and engaging way so that they would not find them particularly hard to understand or, most importantly, take part in.

Reflection:

Neema talks about her experience with the process of documentary production and the key steps she took when making a radio documentary. First she planned the process and laid out the steps she was required to make. Her writing tells me she was excited to be doing this, as it was something she had never done before and she loved working on something new. She saw it as an opportunity for learning and practicing some of her skills, including her decision-making skills. She researched her ideas and she wrote about how important it was to learn everything possible about the documentary subject before making her plan. The plan she created for her project included something unique she developed herself, which was to give her actors the chance to speak for themselves without her interrupting them.

Given my own experience working with groups and getting people to engage, I think this was the right thing to do. It gives a voice to those less heard which is important when examining people's lives, as Neema was doing in her piece. It is also a good way to show you respect what people are saying. Neema understood the link between respect and communication, and she believed that interrupting is not only a rude thing to do, but it discourages people from sharing their own version of the truth.

Many people, including myself, have experienced feelings of dismay when they are interrupted in the middle of an important thought or a conversation. Disturbing someone when they're talking isn't recommended; however, there are situations that call for speaking up and ways to interrupt that aren't rude and disruptive. Neema would have said that we need to give everyone a chance to speak.

She created a shot story, wrote a script, started shooting, began to edit and finished her piece by checking legal and copyright issues. There were some challenges during the process; for example, participants' schedules sometimes didn't coincide with the plans. Neema evaluated her work and quickly realized that this challenge might make her unsuccessful, and so she decided to do things differently. She contacted a group of people she was interested in and offered them the opportunity do what she called 'freedom of documenting their stories' in her absence. This plan worked for her, and Neema wrote about it and talked about her success with allowing her actors to be themselves. They were not unduly hampered by her presence, which was important for the quality of the stories they were providing. She saw a beautiful outcome, and the process yielded better results from willing participants.

Neema wrote that most of her aims for this research piece were met. Primarily, her aim was to educate and let listeners in on the issues affecting young people's lives in the county of Cornwall. Neema found subjects who talked about the top issues of concern for young people, including:

- coping with stress
- school and study problems (failure to succeed in education system)
- mental health awareness (including depression, anxiety and conduct disorders that were often a direct response to what was happening in their lives)
- body image issues,
- physical health
- family conflict
- financial insecurity (lack of employment opportunities and lack of affordable housing)
- self-harm and suicidal thoughts
- dealing with change, grief and loss
- loneliness

- eating difficulties or emotional difficulties with food
- self-esteem
- identity and confidence
- relationship problems
- understanding behaviour and emotions.

Neema aimed to create debate and open up discussion about important issues in the community.

Obviously, it is worth pointing out that bullying is one of the biggest social issues affecting young people of all backgrounds today. Today, we have sets of professional working to help young people around the world identify issues affecting them and their communities. The aim is to empower them to be able to work together and find solutions to resolve their issues so they can live better lives from young ages. The key point here is that empowerment gives them the strength to become good participants in the communities in which they live. The first crucial step is to identify the problem. The second is to generate participation. The big question is, does it matter? Participation gives an opportunity to young people to define the problems in their own words, to put the problem into words that make it solvable. It makes people think about why it's a problem.

If this area of study interests you, find out what's important to young people and explain what's important from your perspective. The vast majority of young people will appreciate this opportunity, and use it as a tool to brainstorm possible solutions. Evaluate the solutions; work together with the young and invite them to take part in the evaluation, meaning that they get to understand what is working and what is not working. Put the solution into action. Again, evaluate the outcome.

CHAPTER 8

Essay #4: Media Campaign Essay

Social networking sites have become something of a phenomenon in recent years. They have opened up a whole new world for us. They are fun, cool, easy to use, fast and reliable. Most people have stopped texting and sending emails altogether. Most messages are now sent via Facebook. Social networking sites can be defined as websites that allows users to create personal profiles about themselves then chat, discuss and share information with others, such as friends and family, or even strangers. Popular examples of social networking sites include MySpace, Bebo and Facebook.

What these sites do is provide a very easy platform for anyone to use. With just a few clicks, a person can be connected with people from all over the world. Young people are easily attracted to this, even though an increase in use among middle-aged people has been noticed. Most social networking sites offer email-like facilities and a public space to say and comment on anything. Users can add their friends from school, their workplace and other groups or find 'new friends' from practically anywhere in the world. This versatility attracts people. They feel anything is possible online and that they can be connected to anyone, anywhere, whenever they want.

Professor of Cultural Analysis Jim McGuigan says that, "In modern societies a sense of community is elusive, yet a medium like the internet creates the conditions for strangers to meet across space and where the inhibitions of face-to-face communication are inoperative. Dialogue and creative exchange between digitalised versions of the self in Usenet bulletin boards and MUD (multi-user domains) are comparatively undistorted by extraneous power and authority." (1996: 168).

This creates a community faster than it is possible in real life and most young people get carried away. Geert Lovink, founding director of the Institute of Network Cultures, notices "… how remarkable it is that many participants do not perceive blogs and social networking sites such as Orkut or MySpace as part of public life. Online conversations between friends are so intense that the (mainly young and often naïve) users do not realise, or care, that they are under constant observation." (2008: 8).

On computers at home, school, or even on the go on their mobile phones, it's all available everywhere. Most of these social networking sites have a very common feature called the 'status update'. Questions such as 'what's on your mind?' or 'what are you doing?' opens up all possibilities. Even the shyest of people can say anything about themselves and find a whole new world of people who share similar opinions. This way they inevitably attract attention, and it may not be of friends and family only. This makes the options of chatting, posting pictures, videos, and contact information on a public space that everyone has access to somewhat unsafe.

This is where the issue of online safety comes in. It is this information that potential attackers, who may even turn out to be 'friends' online, can use to gradually find out about someone and execute whatever plans they may have to cause harm. This is not only limited to physical harm (like finding out a potential victim's address and getting to them physically), it also includes emotional harm such as the numerous cases of online bullying. With online bullying, people conduct malicious online campaigns against someone based on information they have found out about this person. Online bullying includes intimidation, and hateful and degrading comments.

I developed a media campaign aimed at creating awareness of the risks that come with the use of social networking sites set out to create awareness in young people about the dangers of sharing too much information about themselves online, and opening their world to people they do not know and who they cannot be sure of. The objective of the media campaign was to give young people tips and information on how to be safe, but still enjoy their online social networking experiences. As part of the research for the campaign, I set out to find out what is it that make people so trusting online. According to McGuigan, "We live in a world of globalizing capitalism, of environmental risk and great uncertainty. Therefore there is considerable hope in the sheer fluidity of culture and identity, of the breaking down of old barriers and the opening up of new networks of possibility. In this kind of context, different modes of reasoning perform different functions. Instrumental reason is useful but blind. Ironic reason is fun but irresponsible. Critical reason is vital." (McGuigan 1999: 151).

I also set out to find some of the negative experiences people had as a result of some activities on social networking sites they were not aware would be risky. That was one of the main objectives of the media campaign, along with setting up a blog where I could post this information and articles. This was particularly important, as the campaign's main feature was its online platform.

The other objectives for the campaign were to: find out the risks of publishing one's life online, such as personal pictures, address, phone number; record all information on how to stay safe online; post surveys on the blog for the project; post current events related to the dangers faced if not careful with online activities; find out how (and to whom) people share information with; and, open up comments and allow discussion from people about what they think about these incidents, if they have similar experiences to share, and what they learnt from them. Do they care? Have their online activities changed the nature of their relationship?

I also set out to pose the questions, during these posts, on how the use of social networking sites has changed their lives. The other important thing was to carry out an online survey about online safety and ask for people's personal experiences, if any, on this issue. I also set out to contact an organisation that deals with online safety and related issues and asked them to link to the blog, and I inquired about the various activities they do, and what help they offer young people.

I approached the Falmouth Library and inquired about having them as my client for this project. I chose the Falmouth Library because I reasoned that the library was a free library for anyone in the local area to use and, apart from book services, they also offer free IT services. This was the perfect platform for me to pass my message across because the library is in a position to reach out to young people, mainly because the library's focus is to serve the community by providing knowledge.

The people who use the library's IT services have been offered first-hand information and tips about this campaign which will be beneficial to them in their activities on social networking sites. The library's manager referred me to the IT head, who agreed to let me go ahead with the campaign. She also informed me that most of their IT users do not have access to internet at home and others were new to the whole internet experience. I took this into consideration while doing research for the campaign. Based on my research, the IT head needed me to make posters for the library about how to stay safe online. These posters were intended to draw attention from the young people who use the Library's IT services, and direct them to the online blog I created for the project.

The blog I set up for the campaign was for posting the research I did on the various online safety issues. Each post was followed by a comment session where the discussion could continue. There were also links on the blog to different organisations and events taking place that highlighted online safety issues. I also contacted an organisation that deals with online safety and related issues and asked about placing a link to my blog on their site. I thought this would be particularly important, since the main aspect of the campaign was its online presence.

There was particular prominence raised during anti-bullying week (16th − 20th November), which was set up by MySpace and BBC Radio 1. As a frequent user of MySpace, I linked this to the blog and made sure the readers where aware of this, as most young people use MySpace and listen to BBC Radio 1. The results of the online survey were also posted on the blog.

The questions asked on the online survey were: What are your personal stories of social networking dangers? And what risks/dangers have you come across by using social networking sites? Some of the answers given included people saying that they found certain individuals asking them too many questions about their private lives, and this scared them. Some people pointed out the fact that some individuals were keen on asking them if they would like to meet up, or about places where they usually go out to. I found it very useful to carry out this survey because not only did some of the users offer valuable answers, they also gave tips on how to stay safe online, tips such as never to put your address anywhere on the internet and never to share too much information, like private pictures.

The library offers introductory session to new internet users. Part of the campaign was for me to present the library with the information I gathered so the IT instructors could pass it along to new users so they would become aware of the issues. The IT instructors had 'question and answer' sessions with the new users regarding this issue. I attended two of these sessions. New users were referred to the blog, where they could continue learning about the issue and follow links to other useful and supportive websites, as well as links to events such as the anti-bullying one put on by BBC Radio 1 and MySpace.

The campaign was carried out as per the plan, although there was a slow start to it while I tried to figure out the appropriate client to work with. Since the campaign was set out for an online platform, it was logical to have an online client but I felt it needed a physical aspect to it. It was highly helpful that the Falmouth Library offered introductions to new IT users. This acted as an effective way of publicising the campaign.

I also worked around the fact that there was a National Anti-Bullying week in November and the Falmouth Library had not specifically touched on this issue as of then. This was the perfect opportunity for me to approach them and discuss the campaign, especially considering how effective the library's position in the community is. This created the perfect platform for the media campaign to offer a service to young people in the community through the library.

Reflection:

In her *Media Campaign Essay*, Neema describes how social networking sites have become something of a phenomena in recent years. She gives the examples of MySpace, Bebo and Facebook, all popular sites at the time she wrote her essay. She discusses the type of users, and what the sites mean to people and the community. She declares that social media and social networking is not a bad thing because, "They are fun, cool, easy to use, fast and reliable."

However, the negative experiences as a result of some activities on social networking sites are very important to the discussion. As a young person herself, Neema was part of a generation that, in her words, is, "… easily attracted to social networking sites." She points out that while this is attractive to many people, some are not aware of the risks of sharing too much information.

The aim of Neema's campaign was to find out the risks of publishing one's life online. By collecting firsthand experiences and getting people to share their personal stories about social networking, she hoped to open up discussion and find out what the common issues and problems were. Online security is a major issue affecting many people on these platforms, and it is a still very important issue. People who don't understand how to protect themselves can becomes victims of cyber-bullying, which can be emotionally detrimental and can even cause vulnerable people to commit suicide as a result.

Neema worked on this project during National Anti-Bullying Week in the United Kingdom. She saw this event as a perfect platform from which to launch her project, and approach and discuss online safety as part of the campaign she was doing. This is particularly important to point out, because I see a continuation of this theme from what was written in the previous essay. Bullying and depression are common among young people around the world. Neema thought sharing her concerns about online bullying and how it affects people was important. Sometimes bullying can take the form of online campaigns against people based on information others find out about this person on the web. Neema said, "There was a particularly prominent awareness raised during the anti-bullying week (16th – 20th November) which was set up by MySpace and BBC Radio 1." She felt she was contributing by sharing what she learned about people's common issues, particularly those of young people, with the whole world.

Online bullying is a major problem. It is an ongoing and deliberate misuse of power in relationships through repeated verbal, physical and/or social behaviour that intends to cause physical, social and/or psychological harm. It can involve an individual or a group misusing their power, or perceived power, over one or more persons who feel unable to stop it from happening. While bullying has always been part of the human condition, online it can via various digital platforms and devices and it can be obvious (overt) or hidden (covert).

Bullying behaviour is repeated, or has the potential to be repeated, over time (for example, through sharing of digital records). Bullying of any form, or for any reason, can have immediate, medium and long-term effects on those involved, including bystanders. Single incidents and conflict or fights between equals, whether in person or online, are not defined as bullying.

For the purpose of this book, I would like to say that bullying is 'unwanted, aggressive behavior between people that involves a real or perceived power imbalance'. The behavior is repeated, or has the potential to be repeated, over time. In the schoolyard, kids who are bullied and who bully others often have serious problems that can become generational. What they experience and learn about such behaviour can endure for a lifetime and possibly be transmitted to the next generation. Research indicates that there is a relationship between bullying and brain development that is not natural and is damaging. There have been suggestions about how to reverse the damage in developing brains. For example, intervention such as inviting children to cooperate and think about their actions, is one way. Cooperation is a learned skill and it provides a positive approach to stop children from taking advantage of others who are weak.

In order to be considered 'bullying', the behavior must be aggressive and include an imbalance of power. Bullies always have some sort of power over the people they bully, such as physical strength, access to embarrassing information, or popularity. Bullies always aim to control or harm others. The big question is, are people born to bully? The link between early life experience the need to bully is unclear, though it may have to do with wanting to put inherent pain onto someone else.

Power imbalances can change over time and in different situations, even if they involve the same people. Life experience and personal growth along with changing attitudes can reducing bullying.

Another way to define bullying is that bullying behavior happen more than once, or has the potential to happen more than once. Bullying includes actions such as making threats, spreading rumors, attacking someone physically or verbally, and excluding someone from a group on purpose. According to neuroscience, exclusion affects young people deeply, as they are very wired for social nuances in their brains.

There are many types of bullying. Verbal bullying (saying mean things) includes things like teasing, name-calling, inappropriate sexual comments, taunting and threatening to cause harm. Social bullying, sometimes referred to as relational bullying, involves hurting someone's reputation or relationships and includes things like leaving someone out of an activity or situation on purpose, telling other children not to be friends with someone, spreading rumors about someone and embarrassing someone in public. Physical bullying involves hurting a person's body or possessions and includes things like hitting, kicking, pinching, spitting, tripping, pushing, taking a breaking someone's things, and making mean or rude hand gestures. It can occur anytime and anywhere. Between children, bullying can occur during or after school hours, in the school or on the bus; at home, bullying can occur via parents and siblings, though it may be referred to as domestic abuse.

I have been trying to learn from Neema's point of view about the complexity of this major problem, especially among children and young people. A lot of questions about bullying are still not answered, though there are a lot of recommendations on how to deal with bullying. For example, is it possible to reverse the impact of bullying? I think there is need for direction on how to mitigate the damage caused by this social problem. A social science approach alone is not enough to completely eliminate it. Social science studies human beings and their wellbeing, including social expression and communication; however bullying may have intrinsic roots in the brain, and research indicates a need for a more scientific approach to bullying.

Dr. Sam Goldstein, a certified pediatric neuropsychologist who specializes in forensics, school psychology, child development and neuropsychology, says, "Very clearly bullying has become a topic of interest." He looked into the problem of bullying at schools from a historic perspective to provide a different picture on how people understand bullying. He says that beyond the social aspect of the problem, factors such as the environment where children grow up, and political and economic issues have an impact on shaping bullies. "Childhood aggression, particularly children aggressing against other children, has long been a significant clinical and social problem. Over the past fifteen years the emphasis and focus of this problem has shifted to understanding and preventing a specific form of aggression referred to as bullying," says Goldstein.

Bullying is a world-wide issue and according to Goldstein, "Since bullying involves a bully and a victim, early research has been focused on children falling into one of these two mutually exclusive groups. However, it is now known that there is a third group of 'bully victims' who both bully and are bullied by others. It is estimated between 10 and 30 percent of children and teenagers are involved in bullying, although prevalence rates vary significantly as a function of how bullying is evaluated. Bullying has also been found to increase during the middle school years. It is a problem that is not isolated to specific cultures, but is prevalent worldwide."

Goldstein calls for professionals to re-visit their perception of bullying. He says, "These findings hold significant implications in research and school wide programs. At this point, many of the interventions for general aggression, including bullying, have focused on the individual. Altering the context without a focus on changing individuals and vice versa is limiting an approach."

These words say it all, and the dialogue about bullying continues.

CHAPTER 9

Essay #5: Critical Reflective Document

*H*aving decided to work on an individual project, I started looking at the various productions that I could carry out on my own. As a new writer, I decided to focus on a short format in order to concentrate on my writing skills.

I have always been fascinated by short films and the way in which a theme is able to be communicated in such a short frame of time, using less resources, without losing meaning or falling short of the audience's expectations. I decided to work on a short film project, although at the end it changes into a short radio play as will be detailed hereafter.

I decided to limit the short film's structure to about eight minutes. This meant writing a script with very few characters. I did consider the disadvantages of working on my own and carrying out all the duties myself, such as getting to a point where all this work would get overwhelming, or not having someone offer a different point of view from my own; but I decided to go ahead anyway, mainly because I had never done this sort of work before and I considered this a great challenge and something that would help me gain skills and polish skills gained in the past years at university. I needed to do this to be able to see what I'm capable of, something which I need to realise in terms of my future career prospects. In the process, I hoped I would identify my weaknesses and strengths, and be able to draw upon them in preparation for professional life after university.

The script writing process started with a lot of research on the short film genre. In the past I have watched a lot of short films and I love the concept behind them, although admittedly most of them were very experimental in nature in terms of narrative structure and characterisation. The subjects in these films, as well, seemed limited to either one or two main themes; this way, everything that needed to be told in this short format was able to be told in a short time frame.

I decided to settle for two main characters and work with two locations. I also decided to work with the theme of friendship and emotional instability. The writing process for me was particularly eye opening, as it made me research issues I have never dealt with before, including depression and how it affects people and those around them. This research was important, as I needed it to be able to develop my characters and the way the characters interacted with each other. I was especially keen on the language used in the script as this was, for the most part, a story about the relationship between two best friends. I made it a point to listen in on people's conversations every day, just to get the idea of how the script could be written. It was important for me to get a perspective that was different from my own interaction with my friends.

Listening in on people as they engaged in their natural interactions with each other while out and about in town was very effective. I set out writing a ten-minute script, making sure to take an outsider's perspective. To monitor my progress and writing style, I gave drafts to other people to read (my supervisor, a film student friend and a group of script readers from a writers' website) so they could provide feedback on as I went along. I found feedback very useful, as things I overlooked during the writing process were pointed out to me and I was able to make necessary changes. I was also able to look at the different ways in which the story could unfold. However, it was important for me to have the final word on what I wanted the final product to be.

This process was really important for me, as it especially helped me grow as a scriptwriter and taught me very useful lessons about good scriptwriting. It was during this writing and brainstorming process that the idea of changing the script to a radio play occurred.

During the process of writing the third draft (and after getting different feedback on the style of the writing and piece itself), I decided it would be quite a challenge to present the script visually and that the potential for the final production to be very static, and hence boring, was very high, especially since the two main characters spent most of the time verbally interacting one on one with each other as the story unfolded. Upon changing my format, I had to do a lot of research on radio plays, because as much as I had touched on aspects of radio in the past three years in my courses, I felt I needed to go back to find how effective this would be and how well it would work. I found listening to different radio dramas, past and present, helped me gain perspective on the type of work I could do. This was especially good for me, as I now started considering writing for radio as well, which is a great place to break into writing. In the past, the only writing I thought I wanted to do was for TV. I found the books by Tim Brooke about writing for radio very useful, as they gave practical tips on how to write good radio scripts.

As the radio script progressed, I started looking into a time schedule and, more importantly, looking for actors. Finding actors was the most important aspect of this project and probably the biggest worry for me. I wanted to find very good actors who could use their voices to convey emotion particularly well to get the script off the page. Since that was my main concern, I decided to specifically look for actors who had theatrical experience. I was aware of the possibility of being carried away, and of finding actors who would essentially give an exaggerated performance, and this was a bit of a concern for me. But I went ahead with it anyway, as a convincing performance was key to making the final product sound good.

I found the Cornwall Theatre group very useful and helpful. I was able to communicate with different actors there and, as much as my communication with them was about looking for talent to use in my project, I was able to learn a lot about the different work these actors did. This aspect of organising and communicating with the actors about the kind of skills I needed was very useful, as I realised it was a skill I was very good at. I hadn't done this kind of directing before, and it was very important for me to know that I was very good at this so I could list it as something I might be able to do in the future.

After organising initial rehearsals with a group of actors I had communicated with, it occurred to me finding the best actors for the play wasn't as straightforward as I thought. Although I got two who were both really good for the parts, I had setbacks with one of them not being sure of her schedule, and eventually not being able to make it for the final recording. At this point, acutely aware that time was running out and I could fall short on the quality of actors I needed, I decided to continue looking for actors while setting up the necessary equipment needed for the production.

I did not have any particular budget, due to the small nature of the project, so the only incentive to get actors to agree to work with me was to offer to cater food and drink and, of course, to also offer a copy of the finished project for theirs portfolios. This seemed to work well, as most people were keen to work without a specific budget as long as these things were provided for them.

Finally, I found the actors I needed, though with one of them I had to provide accommodation for a night, but that worked well since I was able to have plenty of time to get to know the type of work this actor did, and by the end of the work the actor became a very good contact. We discussed a project she was working on and she mentioned they needed a co-writer for the script, something I was keen to do. I was glad that I was able to not only find an actor for my project, but someone who was also enthusiastic about similar things.

The process of finding actors, as much as I mentioned that it was something I was surprised to find I was good at, got a bit overwhelming at some points. Although it was possible to accomplish it with this small project, I do believe that if it was a bigger project it would have needed a second person to do it, because that way the different roles would be split between the two of us, making it easier and faster to carry out duties.

When it came to how, exactly, the production process was going to proceed, I started by first recording sound effects. This was important to me, as I needed the appropriate sound effects for the appropriate scenes. I set out to different locations, interior locations, as this was where the setting of the drama took place, and I did a lot of research and experimentation on what type of mics to use before I did the initial recording, as sound quality was very important to me.

The most effective way for me to do this research was to look online and to read books on the different types of mics, and then test out the results myself. If the results weren't as good as I wanted them to be, I went back and recorded again, to find out where the problem was, or I tested out different equipment until I was satisfied with the results. Most of the time I alternated between the Audio-Technica AT804 and the AKG

C1000S mic. Of the two, I found the recordings I did with Audio-Technica to be clearer so I mostly used the files I recorded with this mic. I used the AKG mostly for the studio recording sessions.

I decided initially to do a studio recording session for the main character, specifically to capture those intense emotional moments in her head. I also used the recording studio to record a violinist for music to use in the play (after listening to it I had afterthoughts on how it altered the scene and so I didn't do this, but eventually it was used to introduce and end the piece).

Before using the recording studio for the rehearsals and recording session, I did not have any experience with using the recording studio. Having to do practise sessions and have rehearsals was something that was very important to me, as it enabled me to learn the process of using the recording studio (setting up, using the recording studio software and adjusting mic positions time and again to get the best results). This is something that, if I hadn't decided to work on a radio project, I would not have had the opportunity to learn.

In the recording studio, when the time came to record the main characters' parts, I found that I had to adjust the mic position and actors' positions constantly in order to get the best results. Even though I recorded both actors in the studio, when the time came to listen to the recording and edit, I decided to use only some of that recording and rely on the other recordings I did on-set. The reason for this was that I felt the second actor's studio-recorded version was as good as I wanted it to be.

The violinist was recorded on a different day, and I specifically wanted to use this piece of music as a way introducing the flashbacks, and ending them too; but after thinking really hard on this, I decided against using it and used the music to introduce and end the piece instead.

The flashback idea itself was something that I was completely unsure of, right from the writing process, so I left it hanging right up until the editing process. The reason for this was that I was very concerned that it would be hard for anyone listening to this piece to be able to tell the difference between the flashbacks and the present scenes. At some point during the editing process I made a final decision to remove the flashback scenes all together. The point of the flashback during the writing process was to offer the dramatic turning point of the piece, and provide the main action behind the whole story.

During the early stages of the editing process, I found I had to go back and record some of the sound effects over, as they either didn't fit well with some scenes, or were distorted. The major problem I had with some of files was that the hiss and background noise prevented the main sound from being heard. This was a bit frustrating, but it probably would not have occurred if I had enough sound recording experience and more audio knowledge. Having previously experienced good sound quality with the Audio-Technica mic, I decided to go back and use it to record these sounds again, making sure to repeat if necessary. After a series of rerecording, I got the quality I needed and decided to use these files in the project instead.

I also found that the recording session in the studio was recorded at a very low level, so it was a constant battle to correct the levels. I kept testing what sounded best. I also had to cut out a lot of breathing from the main actor in most of the clips, and this got very tricky as I was left with a lot of blips and clicks. I tried fine-tuning these by adding fades where necessary to provide a smooth transition.

In conclusion, as with everything else, this was a learning process for me. I am glad that I made the decision to work on my own, as I had to really stretch myself in every way possible. I also got the opportunity to improve some skills I had only just touched on in the previous years. By working alone, I was able to be directly involved in the project, make my own decisions and move at a pace I felt was best for me. I'm aware that the preferred choice for most people would be a team in order to get input and different perspectives on things, but this wasn't an issue for me as I had a range of opinions and perspectives from my supervisor and friends. So everything, in my opinion, was well balanced. As this was my project, I needed to be in control of it myself. As mentioned earlier, I had not had the opportunity to work on a project by myself and I wanted to do this as a way of challenging myself and also of seeing what I was capable of. I wanted to identify my weakest and strongest areas in preparation for professional life after university.

Although I gained a lot of skills and experience from this project, in the future I would like to focus on scriptwriting, and managing and directing actors, as those are the two areas that I enjoyed most. Those are also the areas that I have, perhaps, learnt a lot more about than I did in the past three years.

One of the main things I would have done differently with this script is to remove the flashback scenes from the beginning in order to prevent the uncertainty during the editing process, and introduce one or two more characters to further develop the main ones, especially the supporting one. I would also focus more on introducing the man who was responsible for the problems the main characters had, leading to the brief bad patch in the relationship with the main character's best friend. This way, I would not have had to worry about how to make the audience understand when a flashback was occurring.

The other thing I would have done differently would be to not record any of it in the recording studio (except for the music) and to go direct to a field recording instead. This would certainly have helped with the issue of sound effects not being very effective, as they would all have been recorded on-set, and therefore the problems experienced with distorted sound effects and hiss would be eliminated. It would also have been good to capture the atmosphere of the whole location itself.

Another thing I would have done differently would be to make sure to listen to all the recorded material several times on different equipment to make sure the quality wasn't lost, as this would have saved time spent trying to correct some of the mistakes in the editing process.

The overall piece itself works, but perhaps the most important part for me in the project was the writing process and the management process. As mentioned before, those are areas I will be focusing on.

Reflection:

Throughout this essay, Neema continue to express her passion for the work she is doing. Neema hoped the training she was getting would help her identify her weaknesses and strengths, and that she could draw upon this in preparation for her professional life in the future after university. She was open to learning opportunities, and getting feedback on the style of her writing and producing activities.

Writing about real life, and using real voices was important to her. Neema believed that writing was a tool to help people tell the stories that matter to them, and she solicited voices that often remain unheard. I call this experience 'the beauty of writing' simply because I think that it is a beautiful thing to help people be heard by writing their stories.

Writing embodies the primitive art of expression, which engenders an individual to expand upon intellectual thought. As a medium of reflection, similar to that of art and music, writing endows humanity with the ability to contemplate multiple aspects of life. Neema learned from her writing practice that writing is not a luxury, but a necessity that enriches one's psyche. She brought up the importance of brainstorming during the writing process and pointed out the importance of feedback in order enhance writing quality. She also discussed taking time for reflection and, as with all art forms, points out that the mastery of writing requires patience and practice.

What makes good writing beautiful? As I read Neema's essay, I became aware that Neema talked and communicated very well. To her, writing was a process of evolution. Nothing can be more vital to writing than the writing itself; how much and how frequently we write. There is no right way to write. Writing glows when the words create images in the mind. Neema provided images that presented richness and texture. Her expectation was that her audience, reading an answer to whatsoever question they had, should be able to transport their reading experience through a maze of flickering images.

Because she was writing for radio, Neema made sure her work would sound beautiful by using a straightforward vocabulary and choosing nouns and verbs for expressive qualities. She also paid a lot of attention to the sound generated by the rhythms created by the syntax she was using. She said, "I started by first recording sound effects," which was one layer of the final piece.

I have always felt that everything can be written beautifully, provided we have a good heart and we nurture a beautiful mind. Nurturing a mind means to do a good amount of reading of good quality writing. Good writing, to become beautiful writing, needed to be fed by good reading. Diversity and depth of reading determines the extent of beauty we are able to achieve in our writing. Neema achieved a certain beauty in her writing is with subtle communication and a clear, concise way of stating things.

Although there are always challenges during the process of writing, one thing Neema was good at was paying attention to audience expectations. As she put it, "I have always been fascinated by short films and the way in which a theme is able to be communicated in such a short frame of time, and with less resources without losing any meaning or falling short of the audience's expectations." What she meant is that it is important to deliver quality, no matter how small a project.

Neema touched on things she would have done differently given more knowledge, resources and time. Listening to the recorded tracks on multiple systems before final edits was one thing she would have done differently, as different equipment and recording procedures yielded different results. Another thing was to tailor her writing to radio more effectively from the beginning so she didn't have to backtrack in the editing process. She made it clear that correcting mistakes is a process that she learned from; however, she would do things differently and more efficiently if she were to repeat the project.

Neema's self-evaluation indicates a high level of maturity and depth for a person her age. She believed it is very important to encourage the audience to participate emotionally in the artwork they are enjoying, and so she took care to make her pieces accessible.

I believe we all have our own library of research in our memory banks and it can be brought into our consciousness by good artwork, such as good writing. It is like hidden treasure and exploring that hidden treasure is not just exciting, but a fascinating journey. It would be wonderful to hear your side of story about what good writing means, and how good writing can be turned into beautiful writing.

CHAPTER 10

Essay # 6: Feasibility Studies Report

Introduction

*I*n the following feasibility studies report, I will explain all the different categories and subcategories that I've done research on (in terms of context and content) as I prepare for the production of my proposed programme.

Research is a very important part of project development because:

- It provides information on what the viewers are interested in, therefore helping prospective programme makers concentrate on an area that is highly marketable.
- It enables one to gauge the current issues and trends, therefore prospective programme makers are able to make programmes that are relevant to current times.
- It provides the prospective programme maker the opportunity to evaluate what resources are

required for a particular programme and how to go about acquiring funding for these particular resources.

- It provides the prospective programme maker the opportunity to find out what various commissioners are seeking and what criteria needs to be met for a proposed programme to be successful.

- It provides the opportunity for prospective producers to find out what kind of production team they are going to need and where to find this in advance.

- It introduces prospective producers with past projects that are similar to what they want to do, so they can learn from these projects and see how it is done.

The main objective is to have a finished production that:

- Is relevant to contemporary lives with the issues they deal with.

- Pushes boundaries when dealing with very controversial issues.

- Challenges the viewers' perceptions of the world around them.

- Is entertaining and extremely thought provoking.

- Is unique.

- Offers a different perspective on how it tackles various moral issues.

- Is real and reflects what your average person goes through.
- Is easily watchable.
- Is easily understood and interpreted.

The programme also seeks to offer an audience a twist and leave them wondering 'what if?' or lead them to have discussions with each other on what would happen if their roles were reversed with those of the characters.

Genre and Format

Generically, I would classify this programme as a short drama. This is fittingly so because basic elements of the drama genre are going to be in use. These elements are dialogue, action and gesture (the various expressions and emotions shown by the characters).

The contemporary issues raised in this programme are also very relevant to most of the drama audience who, as much as they seek entertainment, also like to be engaged in thought-provoking debate, especially debate that deals with contemporary issues. Generic clarity is important to broadcasters because it helps them allocate different time slots for different programmes and therefore enables them to captivate different kind of audiences. This can lead to a boost in ratings and can raise the prominence of their particular broadcast station.

Commissioners seek drama that is relevant to our contemporary lives, with the strongest and most original stories. Drama that is fresh, surprising, debate-provoking, audacious and entertaining is appropriate. Examples of formats currently commissioned include:

- Serials at 2100: could range from 2 × 90' to 6 × 60' and be either period e.g. or contemporary.
- Single films at 2200: A broad variety from holiday events to contemporary authored pieces.

Or

- Series that are 8 X 60 minutes in the first run.
- Half hour or less runs.

Narrative Synopsis

A young woman is sexually assaulted by a masked man. As a result, she falls into deep depression and starts consulting a psychiatrist to help her understand what she is going through, and to help her find a way of healing and feeling better. The woman, however, finds herself constantly going back to the events of that dreadful day. As these flashbacks progress, she finally realises that the man responsible for the attack is her ex-boyfriend. She then sets out to get revenge.

This program has the ability to engage its audience emotionally, because it deals with sensitive issues that the audience is likely to be aware of. Looking at the prominent themes (depression, sexual violence and revenge) it can be noted that these themes are recurrent in our society. Even though most of the audience might not have been affected directly, they are likely to know someone who has or are likely to have gone through a different and lesser scenario. Some might have known depression as result of the loss of a loved one, or loss of a job (especially relevant in current times as the economy rates as the most important issue for many people, overtaking crime, according to Ipsos MORI), or through a broken relationship (or the end of one); some might have wanted to seek revenge for something as little as being hurt by another person's careless words. This makes them relate to the story.

Characters

- *The once 'normal' and average young woman:* She is now withdrawn as she tries to bring her life back together. She does not agree with some of the things that her psychiatrists suggests, so she retreats into the confines of her mind as she tries to understand what happened to her.
- *The masked man.* He is responsible for the attack on the young woman. He remains unknown for most of the programme, only referred to by the young woman, her best friend and the psychiatrist.
- *The young woman's best friend.* She appears to have a very sunny and optimistic disposition. She encourages the young woman to do things that make her 'happy' so that she can forget what happened.

Each character in this programme engages the audience and drives the narrative. The audience is

able to follow along with interest as they ask questions
such as:

- Why did the masked man attack the young
  woman?
- What is she hoping to achieve by going to see
  the psychiatrist?
- Who is the masked man?
- What would I do?
- What if he didn't bother to disguise himself?
  What would her reactions have been?
- Would her behaviour have been different?
- Why is the attacker's identity so important
  to her?
- Why does the psychiatrist insist that she forget
  about it?

The above questions are likely to lead to thought-
provoking debate and make the audience ponder these
highly sensitive issues.

The programme also creates curiosity within the
audience as it progresses since they, along with the
protagonist, want to know why she keeps going back to
that event. Some may find the attacker very mysterious
and may choose to focus on that and wait to see if his
identity will be revealed in the end, and maybe also his
motives. Other will be entirely focused on the girl and
be solely interested in her journey of recovery.

These characters push the story and keep the
audience on its edge as they waits to see what happens

next. It is all the above, therefore, that makes the programme very believable and relevant.

LOGLINE

A young woman slowly realises who is responsible for a brutal attack on her. She then sets out to get revenge.

SYNOPSIS

A young woman is sexually assaulted by a masked man. As a result, she falls into deep depression and starts consulting a psychiatrist to help her understand what she's going through. The woman, however, finds herself constantly going back to the events of that dreadful day. As these flashbacks progresses, she finally realises that the man responsible for the attack is her ex-boyfriend. She then sets out to get revenge.

CHARACTERS

Dawn: 24, medium built. Depressed and closed off.

Alexis: Dawn's best friend. A 25-year-old, cheerful and easygoing woman.

Doctor: Helps Dawn.

Mark: Dawn's ex.

Challenges Dawn Faces: How she gets out of the situation

The contemporary issues raised in this programme are relevant to most of the audience and society in general who, as much as they seek entertainment, also like to be engaged in thought-provoking debate, especially debate that deals with contemporary issues.

Resources: Location and Talent

For this proposed programme, only four actors are required. This means it will be relatively easy to find actors who can do this. I believe offering to cater to any of their needs during the shooting of this programme will motivate the actors to want to take part in this programme. Forming a very close relationship with them, as well as explaining to them in detail my vision for this programme as a director, will help them thoroughly understand the roles they will be getting into and make the whole production experience personal for them.

Due to the short nature of the programme and the content of the story, the location of this programme will not very hard to find and neither will it be expensive to facilitate. We have the young woman shown in the confines of her home most of the time (symbolic to the mental confinement she has created for herself as she grapples with depression and seeks closure); then we have the only external location, where the attack takes place.

The plan for the programme is to use a minimum amount of music because it is important to tell the story mostly through the visuals. I have been looking for a composer (non-professional) who would be willing to compose something short, if only to set the mood of the story.

Budget

A budget has not been drawn for this programme but a rough idea has been made, mainly because I believe it is important for the script to be finished so that I am able to determine the duration, the props needed (and whether they need to be bought or can be improvised) and consider all the final changes that can occur.

Using the rough guide however, I have determined that I will not incur huge expenses in making this proposed programme. As this will be a self-funded project, daily reviews will be made to make sure what is needed in terms of expenses is updated.

Compliance and Technology: Editorial compliance

Every programme made for particular broadcasters must adhere to the specific guidelines of that broadcaster: *Editorial Guidelines and Credit & Branding Guidelines* (BBC); *Compliance Manual* (Channel 4); and Ofcom's *Broadcasting Code* are examples.

Technical Compliance

Every programme made for a particular broadcaster must comply with that broadcaster's technical specifications to ensure it passes a technical review.

A few guidelines of what commissioners require of programmes in this genre in terms of the technology and programme delivery, as found out during my research, include:

Channel 4

It's my responsibility to:

- Be aware of important guidelines such as guidelines on photo sensitive epilepsy (PSE).
- Make sure to avoid aspect ratio errors.
- Be aware of the number of breaks allowed for a particular programme. The number of breaks is regulated by Ofcom and should not be deviated from.
- Make sure the editorial content of the programme is approved or corrected before technical review to avoid the process having to be repeated.

BBC

- Programme tapes must be delivered at the correct duration—this is essential in order to ensure that schedules can be made to work to time.
- Programmes delivered which are not at the correct duration will be returned to the programme department or company for re-editing to the correct length and will require

a new transmission review and copies to be re-run at production expense.

Production

The production team available at the moment for this project has the required skills for this kind of production; however, for the production to take place in effective time there is a need to bring in an extra person or two, especially during the shooting day. This will help things to move faster and get done well within the given timeframe, or earlier. It will also make sure the work is evenly distributed so that none of the production team has their hands full with so many things at once that they end up loosing concentration, which might lead to sub-par work—or impatience with the actors and therefore loss of motivation for them—or lack of trust in the production itself.

I am looking at various examples of similar programmes online and trying to find out how they went about their production, especially with regard to the number of crew they had and the amount of time it took them to finish the production. The BBC's Film Network site has proved to be a very useful resource for this kind of research, with its many examples of cutting-edge short drama and detailed information for aspiring programme makers.

Audience

The Broadcasters Audience Research Board is the organization responsible for providing the official measurement of UK television audiences. The audience is likely to be interested in watching a programme if it touches on issues that affect them in their daily lives. I feel this programme will make them alert and stir interest due to the issues raised.

Reflection:

What is feasibility study report? It is a study of whether it is possible to get something done within certain times and budgets. Neema outlines the procedure and the path for the program she created and talks about her project and how she aims to engage her audience. She writes honestly about her intentions and the challenges she might encounter when creating the production she has envisioned. She prepares herself for the production by focusing on the methods most suitable for project development at that particular time. Her feasibility study summarizes her analysis and evaluations, as well as proposed solutions to potential problems. She identifies whether the project is really feasible, cost-effective and achievable.

Neema also talks about some of the issues she might encounter when she starts producing this particular program, as well as why she chose drama as her genre. I came understand how important dialogue, action, gestures and emotions shown by characters are to Neema. Genres are important thing to broadcasters, because it helps them allocate different time slots for different programs, enabling them to captivate different kinds of audiences. This can lead to a boost in ratings and enhance the prominence of particular broadcasting stations.

Neema chose her topic because it is both contemporary and a universal theme. Neema talked about relevant drama. She said the audience would seek entertainment, but she also pointed out that the audience likes thought-provoking debate. I was fascinated by how Neema planned her production. She included a few things in her long list of things to do, and one of the things was addressing the 'relationality' of the program. She highlighted this as number one thing to do on her do list and chose her topic specifically to be 'relevant to contemporary lives'.

Neema felt her proposed program would engage an audience. "I feel this program will make them alert and stir interest due to the issues raised," she said.

Neema wrote about challenges she expected to encounter when creating her production. Her essay provides evidence of her ability to prepare and produce a program as a director and producer. She carefully wrote all the steps, including the purpose of the program, and the structure and content. Her writing proves that she was equipped with the knowledge, skills, and ability to bring her production to life. She compared her project with past projects that were similar to what she wanted to do, and she talked about the learning experience this was for her. This is a clever approach to project management and development.

Neema clearly understood and was able to differentiate the role of the characters she was writing about from the role of audience. She explains her expectations from the program; for example, she talked about the possibility that the program would create curiosity within the audience as it progressed, since they would want to know more but would have to wait and see what happened next.

Engaging an audience is very important, and Neema talked about how to achieve this goal. She wrote about what the commissioners at networks are seeking, and that they want drama that is relevant to our contemporary lives, and only the strongest and most original stories. Each character in each program must be strong and engage the audience, and then the audience are will follow the story with interest. Neema provides a long list of questions she hopes the audience will formulate and said she hoped they would lead to thought-provoking debate about some highly sensitive issues. She finished her essay by saying that audience questions are important because it means the program is believable and relevant. All appropriate aspects of a good feasibility report are in this essay.

Feasibility reports are paper examinations of whether a particular project is possible, given certain constraints. These constraints could be anything: financial, social, practical, environmental, technical, legal, or any number of other things that could make it impossible or impractical for a project to go ahead. Project management and development, not only in the media and entertainment industries but in the business world as well, all require feasibility reports.

Feasibility reports include an introduction, a problem and a proposed solution. Neema started by discussing her proposed project and its background. In the introduction, which flowed well into the background section, she gave important contextual information. She also included an overview of audience expectations, the history and context of the problem, important technical details, and other information important for understanding whether her project was feasible or not.

Neema talks about her desire to present contemporary issues that are likely to lead to thought-provoking debate and make the audience ponder highly sensitive issues. She also talks about requirements for making the production a reality. This section is sometimes called the 'criteria section', because it includes descriptions of how the writer is evaluating the feasibility of the proposed program. For example, Neema talked about using only four actors for her program, and she evaluated her movie based on cost, environmental impact, and other important criteria. She also wrote about how she would go about evaluating the proposed program. For example, the program experience was good because it was a learning experience. She got many good ideas about how to execute her plans by learning from similar programs.

Finally, in the 'final opinion' section, explicitly states why she thinks her proposed movie is a good, and feasible, idea. She also talks about what she will do next, saying she is looking at examples of similar programs online and trying to find out how they went about with their production so that she can streamline her own processes.

CHAPTER 11

Essay # 7: Media in the Celebrity Culture Sphere

*N*eema did a lot of research and reading. She was well-prepared. Below is an image of some notes she made about this essay, which was her dissertation.

February 2010
BA (Hons) Broadcasting

Media in the Celebrity Culture Sphere

Submitted by Neema Mkwelele to University College Falmouth towards the degree of Bachelor of Arts by undergraduate study in Broadcasting.

I certify that all material in this dissertation which is not my own work has been clearly identified as such and that no material is included for which a degree has previously been conferred on me.

Signed: *Neema Mkwelele*

★★★

TABLE OF CONTENTS

MEDIA IN THE CELEBRITY CULTURE SPHERE

Introduction

"There are the snobs who pretend they are not interested in celebrity culture and are too busy listening to Radio 4; I mean, they are liars but you don't really need to worry about them. Then there are quite a lot of people who think that celebrity culture is of immense and vital importance to their lives and the world. Then there's a certain group of people who might know deep down that it is a load of meaningless bollocks, but they unashamedly love it."

> *- SAM DELANEY, editor of Heat magazine. The Guardian, Monday 18 January 2010.*

In this dissertation I will seek to identify the role that the media plays in celebrity image making and subsequently the power it has on influencing and fuelling the public's obsession with famous individuals, something Gamson refers to as 'the negotiated celebration' (Gamson 1994). Additionally, I will seek to identify the different ways in which the public reacts to this trend whilst highlighting other key factors that facilitate this obsession and the predominant ideologies that influence this.

Celebrity: the state of being famous or a celebrity, an individual who is famous.

Celebrity is something that we hear about all the time. Individuals can be famous for a number of reasons. They may have certain characteristics that the public finds unique or they may have made extraordinary achievements. Of course there are the other individuals who become famous merely by association or birth.

It is these factors that make certain individuals stand out and acquire celebrity status. As these individuals' celebrity status continues to be projected, the public's interest in them continues to grow. Suddenly their lives become of immense importance and the public becomes curious. By its nature, the public is, "Loosely organised through communication surrounding an issue, it includes both active and passive strata, it changes in size and shape as it develops, and it passes into and out of existence along with an issue." (Price 1992: 33). So, as much as the public becomes addicted to this celebrity frenzy, that state is not constant. It is subject to change with a number of prevailing issues, such as when the media ceases to 'publicise' a famous individual.

Herein I challenge the claim that all members of the public in one way or another simply can't resist the allure of celebrity. Rather, it is important to note, not everyone shares this thought of celebrity as unique individuals who need to be adored. Some brush it off as voyeurism and therefore deem it rather irrelevant to their lives. These members of the public mostly react negatively towards this phenomenon (especially when it is clear that it is perpetuated by the media) by complaining about how celebrities are often bad role models to members of the society and that most of them are in fact just vacuous individuals with no exceptional talent. Whatever way you look at this structure, famous individuals provide something for the public to talk about. Numerous factors contribute to the prevailing of celebrity culture today, the media's role being very significant in influencing this obsession with famous individuals.

This is certainly solely due to the fact that the media's role is to disseminate information to society. Most of the information the public receives comes from the media. There has always been a debate surrounding the issue of how this information is disseminated and by who, with Marxist theorists asserting that what the media does is disseminate the ideology of the members of the society who are in control, so that the average individuals who have no control have no other option but to adhere to that ideology (Marx and Engels 1947). There are instances, however, of when individuals in the public who have no control decide to ignore what the media feeds them, as will be shown hereafter. This is usually displayed by a collective diminishing disinterest.

Historically, individuals were revered by society for their significant achievements. Today however, it is considerably easier for anyone to be a celebrity. Mole observes that, "By the end of the eighteenth century it became possible to be famous simply for being yourself." (Mole 2008: 347). Individuals can carefully manipulate the public by using the media (in this case the media is also cleverly manipulating the public) to gain celebrity status. The media is aware that the public is fascinated by individuals of great renown. This brings us to the question of what exactly influenced society's fixation with celebrities in the first place?

Arguably, society's obsession with famous individuals is a result of these individuals' charismatic natures. The public looks at these individuals as unique beings who, in one way or another, seem to live lives that most people desire but cannot attain. These individuals seem to embody what perfect human beings should be, and they have riches, beauty and what appears to be an existence free of worries. They have people who do everything for them and they seem not to work very hard like the average person does. They are seemingly invincible and infallible. However, the fact that this is how they *seem* does not make celebrities mistake free; it just an image they put forward. It is perceived reality, and a performance specifically staged to create fame and money for an individual, something which the public often seem not to understand or accept.

Mostly, whenever celebrities do something or behave in a manner that is contrary to what is expected of them as celebrities a backlash from the adoring public always follows, proving that as much as celebrities may want to bask in the glory of their celebrity status and feel special, it only public interest that makes them famous. This may cease to be so if the public decides they are not worthy of adoration; therefore, it is in the interest of celebrities to keep and maintain an image that will continuously appeal to the public. With this in mind, celebrities hire publicists who work with the media to ensure their image is the kind of image the celebrity wants portrayed. Sometimes, however, the public's interest or disinterest in a famous individual is not determined by the media, no matter how much effort is being made to manipulate the individual's image.

Chapter One: Retracing the history of celebrity culture

Since the media is aware of the public's fascination with celebrities and uses this for its own gain by creating famous individuals (to make profit and increase an individual's celebrity status), the key question is, how did society's fascination with famous individuals come about? Why does society feel the need to celebrate certain individuals? The individuals that society has revered have gone through many changes over the ages. As introduced earlier, in the past individuals become famous because of the genuine talents they possessed and their tremendous achievements. Individuals also became famous for the good that they brought upon the collective society. During ancient civilisations such as the Roman civilisation, society revered people like athletes for their genuine talent and what seemed like superhuman strengths, or religious figures who they felt were their only connection to God. The traditional concept of celebrity at that period in time was based around the acknowledgment of virtue. The way in which an individual became famous nevertheless gradually began to change.

The Renaissance period brought with it the printing and publishing industry, which led to the mass production of books, newspapers and magazines. As McQuail states, "The history of modern media began with the printed book." (McQuail 1983: 18). Printed books increased literacy rates for the common people and information was then easily disseminated to the masses. The public was now able to read about the people they adored. As information about the celebrated became readily available to the public, more people started idolising these famous individuals as a result of their great and seemingly perfect lives getting publicised by the media to the masses. No longer was society interested only in athletes or religious figures that brought them close to God. The public became intimately aware of the private lives of these individuals. It was that reawakening that marked the beginning of the celebrity worshipping frenzy. Print media then expanded into film and film stars were born. They were glamorous individuals and they fascinated the public with their glamour. As the rise of radio and television occurred, the public not only increased their celebration of these stars but they also extended their affection to musicians and the presenters who were brought into their private worlds.

As Marshall explains, the obvious and omnipresent function of television made the public associate more with these celebrities (Marshall 1997: 121). The TV set was always there in their living room. McQuail explains that, "Television has both a domestic and collective character that seems to endure." (McQuail 1983: 32). People could switch it on any time they wanted to and they would instantly be connected to famous individuals. This made the public feel extremely close to the stars.

With the rise of the internet, things changed rapidly. Information was able to be shared at a very high speed through the use of email, weblogs, discussion forums and chat rooms. This made celebrity news and gossip readily available to anyone who wanted it. Celebrity blogs sprang up and fed the public's craving for celebrity news. It was easier than ever for people to know what their favourite celebrities were up to.

Key in this was the public's need to know the details of celebrities' private relationships with people, especially those of a romantic nature. This clearly illustrates man's nature of needing something to talk about. Mobile phone technology also played a major role during this information age. People were able to go online on their phones whenever they wanted and find out information about celebrities.

We now have numerous ways in which news about famous individuals can reach us. The media has ensured that we continue to receive information about celebrities, even when we really do not wish to do so. Tabloid newspapers, which continue to be the best-read newspapers in Britain (Johansson 2008), such as The Sun and celebrity gossip magazines such as Heat, have all gone interactive in order to maximise the way celebrity news and commentary reaches the public. The Sun has an online platform where people can read about celebrities, take part in quizzes about them and even engage in discussions (via comments and forums). Heat magazine not only has an online platform like The Sun, but also a radio station for the hopelessly addicted. This constant circulation of celebrity news in the media makes people aware of it. It is there and they are constantly bombarded with it.

Chapter Two: Creating and producing the celebrity

The constant portrayal of celebrities in the media does not stop only at interviews about their lives, but ventures into having celebrities appear on TV shows and sometimes even take part in presenting their own shows, or writing magazine articles. One has to wonder about the exact position of media in all of this. Conspicuously, the media deliberately produces celebrities and then markets them to the public, the ultimate goal being higher ratings and revenues for media companies while the celebrity's profile is raised.

This is what Rojek (2001: 121) refers to as 'staged celebrity'. Staged celebrity is defined as the calculated technologies and strategies of performance and self-projection designed to achieve a status of monumentality in public culture. In cases where these technologies and strategies are successful, the achieved celebrity may acquire enduring iconic significance.

The invention of the reality TV genre provides the perfect opportunity for media companies to produce celebrities for the public consumption. The public looks at reality TV as something that is different, reading it as 'realistic', with the power to give average members of the public the chance to appear on TV and be famous just like the individuals they adore. Judging by the reception reality TV has received (Hill 2005) it is indicative of how naive the public is of the tactics broadcasters use. Broadcasters clearly exploited this belief by creating shows that claimed to be real and for the average person, yet in fact ended up making these individuals famous, therefore creating more celebrities for the public to obsess about, and the trend continues. Now the public can't get enough of it. This longing for a taste of the 'real' is symptomatic of a waning sense of reality in the postmodern era (Andrejevic 2004: 8). Each new program of the reality TV genre brings with it a different set of famous individuals. Members of the public, as much as they enjoy watching these individuals, are aware of the possibility of their lives being turned around. They, too, could be on TV and become famous if they wanted. They would be able to emulate the lifestyles of the celebrities they adore.

The media, "Wants celebrities involved with their projects because they believe this will help them attract audiences." (Redmond and Holmes 2007: 193). Media companies are always buying and circulating the images of celebrities, which translates to owning them, even though this essentially refers to the agreements they make with celebrities in the form of signed contracts. Shows such as *Big Brother* and *X Factor* not only make relatively unknown people famous (the participants), they also employ other celebrities (who are of already established fame) in the presenting role or occasionally feature them in various episodes. This raises the profiles of these celebrities. The media is aware that most members of the public will watch these shows to 'monitor' the performance of their favourite celebrities, if not for the participants. Ultimately, the sole decision of who the celebrity will work for lies with the managers and publicists, who in most cases are individuals with very good connections with the people in the media. These are the people who decide what will be good for the celebrity's image, an image that needs to be maintained at all costs in order not to alienate fans, for the fans have been made to believe that that is indeed who the celebrities actually are. They do not realise that it is mostly just for show.

Curran and Gurevitch explain: "The television camera and microphone do not record reality, but encode it: the encoding produces a sense of reality that is ideological. What is represented then is not reality but ideology, and the effectivity of this ideology is enhanced by the iconicity of television by which the medium purports to situate its truth claim in the objectivity of the real, and thus to disguise the fact that any 'truth' that it produces is that of ideology, not reality." (1996: 54).

Managers and publicists therefore make these negotiations with the media and, if they are convinced that working with a particular broadcaster will be good for their clients, they get into a contract with them. It is obvious that the above process is a carefully coordinated one. There is an image to be maintained.

These celebrities might not act in a certain way in their private lives, but since they need to make money and retain their fan base, they adhere to their managers' instructions and also rely on their publicists' image manipulation expertise to portray the best image of themselves to the public. This is in itself a form of production. They are prepared and churned out to the public in a particular image.

The celebrities are aware of the game and they play along. They may be talented, but without a team of people behind them, it is easier for their star quality to wane away in the eyes of the public. This team behind the celebrity is there to ensure they are at the right place at the right time and they are also saying and doing the right things— 'right' according to what the public wants or what the managers, publicists and media people *think* the public wants. Crucial to this is the fact that the managers' and publicists' careers are reliant on how effectively they manage celebrities (Redmond and Holmes 2007: 193).

A good example of production of celebrities by the media is evident in the contestants who take part in the aforementioned shows. These shows follow a now too familiar format. Each show has its season, where everything and everyone is new, because to recycle participants from a previous show would be very boring in the public's eyes. New people have to be brought in. The public has moved on. They want something fresh and new, just like the format of these shows promise: fresh talent. The media in this case continues to churn out celebrities with a very short shelf life just to maintain the public's interest. While some of these celebrities are lucky enough to end up with a very clever team of managers and publicists who will continue to make sure that they remain in the public eye, most of them just fade into obscurity, proving the point that most of these people really had no genuine talent or star quality to begin with. They are just ordinary individuals with a hint of charisma that the media manipulated to the maximum to deceive the public into believing that they were getting their money's worth.

Chapter Three: The allure of celebrity

As clearly stated, the celebrity worshiping frenzy is nothing new. There are numerous reasons as to why society feels the need to idolise some individuals within it, especially today. For instance, if we are to look at the issues of identity and self-esteem in society today, it becomes clear that members of the public feel the need to ascertain if they share certain hobbies or qualities with these celebrities. Since it is highly unlikely that they will achieve this kind of celebrity status, it is important for them feel close to these famous individuals, hence elevating their self-worth. They may also feel that by reading about celebrities' scandals and downfalls that they are somehow better than these people even though they are not as famous as them, because celebrities have always been portrayed by the media as perfect people who live in a world where everything is equally perfect. Finding out about a famous individual's heinous activities is also very exciting. It is interesting and breaks away from the monotony of the idea of a traditional celebrity. They prefer instead to hear about the scandals that befall famous people (Bird, 1997). In this postmodern society (Calinescu, 1987: 134, 135), the social spectrum has become increasingly fractured (McGuigan, 1999). The sense of community that every human being desires has continued to diminish. The individualistic culture, coupled with new technological inventions, has made people less and less dependent on others. Most people thus try to forge a sense of community with other members of the public by becoming obsessed with famous people so that they can have something in common to talk about. The experience itself of knowing that they feel the same way about a celebrity as their neighbour, or that they were at the same location with their neighbour as a celebrity, makes people feel as if they are part of a solid and meaningful community.

Looking at the issue of technological inventions, it's important to note that innovative technology has enabled the media to create and distribute famous individuals very fast, as evidenced in the reality TV format, especially the 'fly on the wall' type. Numerous high-tech cameras in every corner are used to record these events. A program like *Big Brother*, by way of illustration, has 33 cameras in the house and 40 microphones (Channel 4, 2003). This is to ensure that absolutely everything is recorded and transmitted. People sitting at home are fed this information, no matter how little it is, constantly and in one way or another they find themselves getting addicted to it. It is created that way by broadcasters to lure people in.

Information about celebrities, or soon to be celebrities, is everywhere. Talent competitions follow the same format. Cameras and microphones are used to record each participant's reaction. The audience is bombarded by this information and unknowingly begin to form 'relationships' with these people. They want to know their life story. What did they do before they decided to enter the talent competition? What are their hobbies?

At this point, the media has already drawn a line between these contestants (soon to be celebrities) by implying that their stories are more important than of those of the people sitting at home watching. The numerous cameras, microphones, special editing styles and background music all act to emphasise this point. It should also be considered that members of the public obsess about celebrities for the mere fact that they want to fit in. A particular group of friends might get together and start talking about the latest celebrity scandal; what better way than to be aware in advance so that they one can fully participate in the ensuing discussion?

Chapter Four: Case Study
Kerry Katona: The Making and Breaking Of

Once a member of the girl band Atomic Kitten and then the wife of Brian McFadden, a member of the highly successful band Westlife, Kerry Katona was consequently the winner of the ITV reality programme *I'm A Celebrity...Get Me out Of Here!* She's now gleefully ridiculed in equal measures by both the media and the public. One need not be surprised by this kind of behaviour by the public because, as is often the case, the media played a role in making her famous and is now playing an equal role in ridiculing her for financial gain.

In order to articulate what went wrong, it is important to track the way in which she became famous. She came into prominence as a member of Atomic Kitten, even though her membership was short-lived and her talent slightly questionable after she admitted that she didn't actually sing (Reynolds 2003). This in itself proves that instant celebrity does not require any sort of special quality, effort or skill.

She left the group but, unlike so many others seeking fame, continued to remain in the limelight, mainly due to her well-publicised marriage to Brian McFadden and her appearance in various light entertainment TV programmes.

The downturn of events for her began after the divorce from McFadden. The meagre divorce settlement she received from her ex-husband, who admitted to squandering a lot of the money he made with Westlife, did not work in her favour in terms of her career as a celebrity, for it was against what the public is accustomed to seeing from famous individuals. In order to rate a famous individual's celebrity status highly, they expect a huge payout. Celebrity, as much as it is about fame, is also about money, at least that's what the media has made it look like. Moreover, money is essential for celebrities to buy the best celebrity making team, managers and publicists, who will then work to maintain the image of the celebrity or change it to suit a particular interest that they would like to exploit. Katona's image hasn't been the exact embodiment of what the public expects of celebrity. With celebrity, they expect money, class and intelligence; it is part of the reason they have always revered the famous, because the famous are distinctively set apart from the average members of the public. Katona, on the other hand, is easily described and distinguishable as an individual who unexpectedly became wealthy and famous. She lacks talent and hails from an unrefined background (she was brought up by a single mother, placed into foster care and she posed topless in her teens). Tyler and Bennett describe individuals like her as 'celebrity chav' (2010: 4). Chav is used as a term to describe, "Young, white, working–class men and women as shiftless, tasteless, unintelligent, immoral or criminal." (Tyler and Bennett 2010: 4).

The celebrity chav is a figure who has become rapidly and unexpectedly wealthy or publicly visible—typically through reality television—and is represented as constitutionally unable to manage this change of circumstance with dignity, sangfroid or prudence. Oxymoronic in terms of an increasingly hierarchized celebrity culture, the celebrity chav is the excessive embodiment of class hatred.

Kerry Katona's marriage itself was questionable, seen only as a matter of image-making and exploiting the public for financial gain and celebrity status, something which McFadden confessed to after their divorce (Metro 2007). Her second marriage was to a taxi driver (who is widely loathed by the public) with whom she had two more children, demonstrating the characteristics of irresponsible motherhood, according to the public (for she could not possibly be a stable and responsible mother by having children with different fathers). Additionally, she confessed to smoking and drinking while pregnant. The public's disapproval of her wasn't helped by the reckless spending on what was commonly perceived as irrelevant and tasteless goods.

The public's consideration of Kerry Katona as a working-class member of society, due to her upbringing, was continually illustrated by these actions. She made money, but did not know what to do with it. She was famous, but did not how to behave appropriately. In this case Katona's spending was a way for her to identify with what the public considered refined and middle class, but since she did not have any idea of what this was, she failed and ended up consuming materials that she was familiar with that were not 'classy', illustrating the link between consumption and identity, succinctly explained by Hayward and Yar. "So encompassing is the ethos of consumerism within (late) capitalist society that, for many individuals, self-identity and self-realization can now only be accomplished through material means." (2006: 11).

From the moment the meltdown began, undoubtedly the public's adoration of her abated, undeniably due to the fact that they finally saw through her and the media gimmicks and realised that she, in fact, had no talent. She lacks the star factor that they are so accustomed to. Further, her choices regarding very important issues in her life have been bad, especially regarding issues crucial to maintaining her celebrity image, such as her appearance (weight gain) which the public ridiculed.

Bordo describes society's association of excess body weight with moral or personal inadequacy, or lack of will (1993: 192). Comments from members of the public vehemently put off by the person she became implied that she was behaving in a manner reflective of her working-class upbringing, as articulated earlier. In other words, it was simply pathological.

It can be argued that it is not Katona's upbringing or social class (implied or otherwise) that is the problem. It is just a matter of the members of the public subconsciously demonstrating their ingrained bourgeois attitudes towards her. These members of the public want to respect her as a celebrity, but they cannot because her tastes and preferences have already been classified as working class, hence she is undeserving (Hollows 2000: 117).

Reasonably, the ruinous events in her life enabled her to remain in the limelight. She still had the chance to appear on TV and declare that her actions were a result of her bipolar disorder, and she continued making TV programmes about her life (MTV's *Kerry Katona: What's The Problem?*, 2009). Bell notes that, "Her career is an ongoing process of managing, repudiating, and creating the scandals that afford her media attention." (Bell 2008). Bell's statement is proved to be true by the reaction some of the viewers of the programme. A viewer on the programme's website declares that Katona is, "... defnitely [sic] wild. She is very fun to watch," (MTV UK, 2009) evidently, illustrating the point that the public demands scandal; they want to sit in the comfort of their homes watching these celebrities make mistakes and feel good about their lives. They want to feel they are better human beings.

The media is aware of this, and caters to this demand by having famous individuals appear in programmes of this nature. This interest can be short-lived, as clearly seen in Katona's case where her last show was cancelled due to a drop in the ratings which evidently includes a range of factors, from the public getting bored of the same antics to the way she was portrayed. The media here is seen to be in control of things. The public acts on the information they get fed by the media.

Conclusion

In conclusion, it is clear that the media plays a big role in celebrity culture. The main reason celebrities have to continually transform themselves (their image) to suit the public's needs is to keep people interested. At the centre of this constant negotiation of celebrity images are managers and publicists. Famous individuals need to constantly have some form of attention on them because, by definition, that is what fame is. There is no point in being famous if one cannot direct attention to themselves via media.

Media disseminates information to the public and publicises celebrities for consumption by the public. It also plays a major role in creating these individuals and it can break them too. The breakdown could be something celebrities start themselves, like getting involved in scandals, but the media will pick up on that and accelerate it further. Whatever way you look at it, the media is always there to influence something, be it bad or good by manipulating the way the public sees things, controversially playing on aspects such as attitudes, trends and characteristics of society. However, the public is not merely passively consuming ideology perpetuated by the media; rather, it is constantly analysing it.

The reality TV genre was considered very innovative and ground-breaking in the beginning, and now it is mostly seen as cheap TV made for members of the public who dream of nothing but a quick shot at fame. However, the public has always been mesmerised by famous individuals. What the media is doing is just providing an easier and more addictive way for the public to idolise them.

Reflection:

This last essay is the core of this book. Neema's analysis of celebrity culture and the role of the media in that brings up interesting points about what society needs to have in common to function as a unit. In a increasingly isolated society, celebrities are one thing we have in common. Neema described the role of media in creating this, saying, "This is certainly due to the fact that the media's role is to disseminate information to society." I agree with the statement; most of information the public receives comes from the media. But that doesn't mean it's good information.

This essay was Neema's dissertation, a requirement for her to complete her Bachelor of Arts (Honours) degree in broadcasting. The choice of this topic was a perfect match for what Neema hoped to achieve in her life. She wanted to learn more about the relationship between the media and celebrity in the context of celebrity culture in the same way she wanted to learn more about her own role in the larger scheme of things, because who are we if we are not the star in our own life?

Neema described what was happening with media, and especially online social media and social networking, in her essays. She takes a look at what it means to be a celebrity and also what it means when your 'star falls' and people turn on you via media presentation of who you are. My perspective is that the media and entertainment industry should take full responsibility for this type of behaviour.

Neema selected demographic celebrities as her demographic group and carefully linked this definition with the role of media. The media's role is to disseminate information to society. Generally, she pointed out that there is a strong relationship between the media, particularly social media, and celebrities, and that economics play a large part in this tie. She brought attention to the fact that celebrities are also used as tools to promote business via social media for the entertainment industry.

Neema also examined the history of this demographic group, calling this 'retracing the history of celebrity culture'. She talked about the process of creating and producing a celebrity as well as the allure of celebrity and what it means to be one. While the concept of celebrity culture is not new, modern technology and a thriving gossip industry have put our fascination with fame into overdrive. I was guided by Neema's writings to pinpoint the relationship between the media and celebrities.

First and foremost, I was interested in understanding the meaning of the word 'celebrity'. Who are celebrities? To me and other people, celebrities are just like us; they're people with problems, who sometimes drink too much, or hit their wives, or have bad relationships—but they do it in the public eye. The illusion that we can get to know these people fuels a lot of subsidiary media enterprises. Celebrity culture is characterized by a pervasive preoccupation with famous persons and an extravagant value attached to the lives of public figures whose actual accomplishments may be limited, but whose visibility is extensive.

Social media channels have given rise to a plethora of role models—both positive and negative—that allow people, especially young people, to find someone that they can identify with. This online celebrity culture has exposed our youth to a world beyond their own; they have role models that appear diverse and authentic. When the relationship between young people and celebrity culture is not positive, it can sometimes cause young people to act out in destructive ways. Social media platforms are not driven by quality of content, but by popularity and surveys have found that young people fixated by celebrity appear to exist in a state of permanent diversion.

Celebrity culture defines thought and conduct, style and manner. It affects, and is affected by, not just fans, but entire populations whose lives had been shaped by the shift from manufacturing to service societies, and the corresponding shift from consumer to aspirational consumer.

I asked myself this question; why do celebrities exist? I learned that where once the famous achieved an almost godlike status, one that seemed impermeable and historical, today celebrity exists for, and by, an information age. In our global and atomized world of bits and bytes, where information is instantly available, massive in its quantities, and as perishable as an electronic image, celebrities help personalize that information. They put a human face on it. However, they are diminished in the process. Information comes at us with incredible speed, in innumerable changing faces and stories, on Court TV, on CNN in 24-hour play. We have far too much information about celebrities these days—their love affairs, their private conversations on cellular phones, the color of their underwear, how many nose jobs they've had, how many intestinal polyps our presidents have had removed.

Another important question is, why does celebrity culture matter? Today, celebrity rules our world. Famous names and famous faces sell us products, push social change and tell us who to vote for. Politics itself has become an exercise in showmanship. The figure of the celebrity politician has become more ubiquitous. To win elections, not only do you have to be intelligent, competent and diligent; you have to look presidential as well.

Celebrity has a second major role: as a weapon of mass distraction. Research evidence and surveys published around the world indicate that people who are the most interested in celebrity are the least engaged in politics, the least likely to protest and the least likely to vote. This appears to shatter the media's frequent, self-justifying claim that celebrities connect us to public life; it's a contradictory way of viewing specific audiences like celebrities. The celebrities you see most often are hawking the most lucrative products, extruded through a willing media by a marketing industry whose power no one seeks to check. This is why actors and models now receive such disproportionate attention, capturing much of the space once occupied by people with their own ideas: their expertise lies in channelling other people's visions.

But the surfeit of information strips the famous of the sacred and heroic—therefore our culture and our own lives—as heroes reflect what we believe is best in us. Yet for every action there is an equal and opposite reaction, and so a certain cynicism has set in among us all, and a rabid fascination not only with the false beauty of the glorified, sterilized celebrity, but also with the dark and seamy underside. I personally believe that we live in a media culture that encourages people to think two different things. One is that celebrities live lives we can't possibly imagine, and they are worthy of our slavish devotion, attention, and respect and the other is that they are all flawed and somehow worse people than us.

In recent years, what it means to be a celebrity has changed beyond all recognition, particularly as a result of social media. But, has it become worse than ever? This is a very difficult question to answer because the very technology that has brought heroes, albeit manufactured ones, into every home has also brought the stark, vivid images of their failures and vulnerabilities and mortality into their bedrooms and living rooms, on television and in newspapers. Neema's case study on Kerry Katona gives a concrete example of the relationship between the media and celebrities, and the media's contribution in influencing and shaping celebrities, their culture and relationships.

CONCLUSION

*M*y life has been filled with a fascination for books and through my years of education, training, and accreditations there has been many opportunities to both read and write. I am not going to pretend that all of those books and readings have been interesting, nor have I managed to retain all of the information that has crossed in front of my eyes, but my reading and writing through the years have built my knowledge base and deepened my love of words and ideas. Reading the words of my daughter further provided emotional insight into a person I loved dearly.

In my work as a social researcher I have often been called upon to provide written reports and documents designed to address social issues, review policies and provide recommendations. Although these have been my primary writing experiences, I knew one day I would want to write something different. So, here I am; I want to write books about my late daughter, Neema.

It came about because I started to think about how to help myself and I was discussing this dilemma with my husband one day. I told him I felt a bit stuck, as I had at least three books in me—yes, I told him that I have three books to write. I wanted to write a book that was informative, shared practical, real-life experiences and was entertaining. The problem was that I was truly lost on how to actually do this. I did not want to proceed with a book aimed at solving social problems that might be boring, nor did I want to put something out there that was so lightweight that I would lose credibility.

My husband asked me, "How about Neema's essays, and a memoir about her life?"

He was right, and I agreed with him totally that this was a good starting point. Movement was required. Enough thinking and worrying about how to write; it was time to just start writing. I decided I would figure out my style as I wrote, rather than wait until I had it all figured out. Once I tossed a few ideas around, I recognized that I needed to start writing about what Neema loved most in her very short life. I started by writing a short story about her, a memoir. Then I felt I needed to focus, and I picked a title to help me get going.

I realized that I wanted to have a book published by the time I was ready to start working on the Neema Edward Mkwelele Wellness Foundation, a book that would fit well with my grieving journey and describe the exceptional purpose of my life, as that was the place all my future books would come from. In order to do this I was knew I had to break out of my familiar patterns of writing, capture my genuine personality and expose my authentic life. So I sat down at the computer and began to write. I did not know what I was going to say, but I began to stumble through it.

This process of collecting and sharing what Neema wrote in her essays was important to me. It allowed me to tell interesting and worthy stories about the human condition using examples from Neema's life and work, because she wrote about the human experience and she wrote the truth. In the essays she wrote, Neema examines, although sometimes very briefly, the attitude and behaviour of people in direct relationship with the media. She brought attention to issues around social media and online activities that are relevant today.

Neema was not just writing her story; her essays emphasized the importance of creating a clear connection between her personal experience and wider culture, and understanding the big picture of issues around the media and online information sharing, and safety, and security.

As I read the essays, I was surprised by my ability to put them together like someone picking a book to read. As I started reading, I found myself creating pictures in my mind, imagining Neema, and asking myself questions about what she might have been thinking as she wrote. Then I asked myself the bigger question, *where did we come from?* This is a question we all ask ourselves as we navigate how we got where we are, and work on ideas to help us in our life experiences. As I learned more about the evolution of media, I also began to ask, *where are we going?* Maybe I just need to live long enough to see what will happen and how the world will unfold.

I tell myself that there is a soft but insistent knock on the door, and we're being told that the future is right here, right now and it's exciting. It's also daunting and frightening because, while I used to think social media was a force for good, evidence says I am wrong. It's clear these platforms create divisions, exploit our insecurities and impact our health. They're as bad as the tobacco industry, and just as addictive. The media shapes our perception of the world and our attitudes, behaviour and future outlook are impacted, regardless of culture, context and languages. People need to be aware of what is being fed to them. Some is truth and some is just a carefully orchestrated dance.

It was important to Neema to invite people to take part in discussions, and she remarkably got incredible results, and as she put it, because people respond well to working with issues that affect their daily lives. This is a clever strategy for community engagement.

With regard to community engagement, I want to tell you about something very dear to me, the Rotarians, Rotary Club members. I am an active member of the Lions Gate Rotary Club, North Vancouver. The Rotary Club has been working to eradicate polio for more than 30 years, and we've made incredible progress in the fight to rid the world of it forever.

I am proud to be a Rotarian because we've helped reduce polio cases by more than 99.9 percent. That's an encouraging figure. The report the Rotarians issued on this says that if all eradication efforts stopped today, within 10 years, polio could paralyze as many as 200,000 children each year. Therefore, the world needs to come together to support and help the Rotary Club and its partners because they can't get to the finish line alone. We're close to eradicating polio, but we're not done yet. According to the Global Polio Eradication

Initiative, there are only three countries that need to finish eradicating polio, Afghanistan, Nigeria and Pakistan.

The Global Polio Eradication Initiative is a public-private partnership led by national governments partnered with the World Health Organization (WHO), Rotary International, the US Centers for Disease Control and Prevention (CDC), the United Nations Children's Fund (UNICEF) and the Bill & Melinda Gates Foundation. Its goal is to eradicate polio worldwide. It's crucial to eliminate polio from the last three countries where it remains endemic and to keep other countries polio-free. From Google search, I have learned that the three countries face a range of challenges such as insecurity, weak health systems and poor sanitation. Polio can spread from these 'endemic' countries to infect children in other countries with less-than-adequate vaccination.

Ending a disease like this around the world requires a lot of work; this is a massive effort, and Rotary and partners can't do it alone. I think people have heard our voice, and I also believe people will join our efforts to end polio. I am writing to tell people reading this book that there is a day called 'World Polio Day'. It is a special day for educating people and raising awareness about this disease. It provides a clear message to all people that we need your voice to help us end polio now.

Interestingly, social media has been invaluable in spreading this message. Why? Because social media is an increasingly effective strategy for charities and not-for-profit organizations to connect with supporters. A recent survey showed that UK charitable organisations have doubled their supporters on key social media channels in the past year. Yet, for many charities, the vastness of the social media landscape is too daunting to venture into.

Free publicity is a benefit of social media. Clearly these organizations rely on public support and so need to find new ways to reach their supporters, potential donors and volunteers. Social media can be one of the most effective ways to build supporters, boost donations, share success stories, network with like-minded organisations, encourage people to sign up to campaigns, recruit volunteers, or demonstrate the impact of their work. It's incredible, and Google search tell me that, with 80 percent of 18 to 24-year-olds and 73 percent of 25 to 34-year-olds using Facebook and Twitter respectively, these platforms are especially relevant to charities keen to engage with a younger generation of supporters.

Rotary is an international community that brings together leaders who step up to take on the world's toughest challenges, locally and globally. Recent major milestones include their work on the eradication of polio. This is one of the Rotary Club's longest standing and most significant efforts, and it's important to talk about and share this achievement.

The history of polio goes back to 1894, when the first major documented polio outbreak in the United States occurred in Vermont. It led to 18 deaths and 132 cases of permanent paralysis. Then in 1905, Swedish physician Ivar Wickman suggested that polio was a contagious disease that could be spread from person to person, and he also recognized that polio could be present in people who showed no symptoms. In 1908, there was a new discovery, and two physicians in Vienna, Karl Landsteiner and Erwin Popper, discovered that polio was caused by a virus. Then in 1916, a major polio outbreak in New York City killed more than 2,000 people. Across the United States, polio took the lives of about 6,000 people, and paralyzed thousands more.

- In 1929, Philip Drinker and Harvard University's Louis Agassiz Shaw Jr. invent an artificial respirator for patients suffering from paralytic polio—the iron lung.
- In 1953, a vaccine developed by Dr. Jonas Salk is declared 'safe and effective.'
- In 1960, the U.S. government licensed the oral polio vaccine developed by Dr. Albert Sabin.
- In 1979, Rotary International began its fight against polio with a multi-year project to immunize six million children in the Philippines. In 1985, Rotary International launched PolioPlus, the first and largest internationally coordinated private-sector support of a public health initiative, with an initial fundraising target of $120 million USD.
- In 1988, Rotary International and the World Health Organization launched the Global Polio Eradication Initiative. There were an estimated 350,000 cases of polio in 125 countries.

- In 1994, the International Commission for the Certification of Poliomyelitis Eradication announced that polio had been eliminated from the Americas.
- In 1995, health workers and volunteers immunized 165 million children in China and India in one week. Rotary launched the PolioPlus Partners program, which enabled Rotary members in polio-free countries to provide support to fellow members in polio-affected countries for polio eradication activities.
- In 2000, a record 550 million children—almost 10% of the world's population—received the oral polio vaccine.

The Western Pacific region, spanning from Australia to China, has been declared polio-free. The Rotary Foundation raised $119 million in a 12-month campaign. Rotary's total contribution to polio eradication exceeded $500 million. Six countries remain polio-endemic; Afghanistan, Egypt, India, Niger, Nigeria, Pakistan.

- In 2004, in Africa, synchronized National Immunization Days in 23 countries targeted 80 million children, the largest coordinated polio immunization effort on the continent.
- In 2006, the number of polio-endemic countries dropped to four—Afghanistan, India, Nigeria, and Pakistan.

- In 2009, Rotary's overall contribution to the eradication effort neared $800 million. In January, the Bill & Melinda Gates Foundation pledged $355 million and issued Rotary a challenge grant of $200 million. This announcement resulted in a combined $555 million in support of the Global Polio Eradication Initiative.
- In 2011, Rotary welcomed celebrities and other major public figures into a new public awareness campaign and ambassador program called "This Close" to ending polio. Program ambassadors include Nobel Peace Prize Laureate Desmond Tutu, violinist Itzhak Perlman, co-founder of the Bill & Melinda Gates Foundation Bill Gates, Grammy Award-winning singers Angelique Kidjo and Ziggy Marley, and environmentalist Dr. Jane Goodall.

Rotary's funding for polio eradication exceeds $1 billion. In 2012, India surpassed one year without a recorded case of polio and was removed from the list of countries where polio is endemic. Polio remains endemic in just three countries. Rotary surpassed its $200 Million Challenge fundraising goal more than five months earlier than expected. In 2014, India had gone three full years without a new case caused by the wild poliovirus, and the World Health Organization certified the South-East Asia region polio-free. Polio cases are down over 99 percent since 1988. It's a very long history of hard work and dedication.

I celebrate the work we Rotarians do, and I am writing this book with pride because I take pride in Rotary contributions. I am happy to share that that Rotary Club took initiatives to work on eradicating polio in poor countries. They raised funds and created a project to immunize children in the Philippines. I also celebrate the fact that this history is a perfect match of this book title. Rotary and partners, social media and celebrities working together to continue the fight of this disease.

About the media and celebrities—it's good to talk about the fact that they give communities millions and millions of dollar to help. For example the Entertainment Industry Foundation serves as a 'gateway to giving' for the entertainment industry, creating and supporting ground-breaking programs that raise awareness and funds for issues that affect millions of people around the world. Celebrities are among those involved in the fight to eradicate Polio around the world.

The Entertainment Industry Foundation was created in 1943 by Hollywood icons Samuel Goldwyn, Humphrey Bogart, James Cagney and the Warner brothers. The Entertainment Industry Foundation has focused on some of the most pressing needs of our time, giving some of the first grants directed to wartime agencies such as the United States Organizations and American Red Cross. They are utilizing the power of the industry to help eradicate child polio and to aid current efforts to raise funds and awareness for critical health, educational and social issues. The significance of this is so huge. I'm calling for all people to passionately bring change to communities and people around the world.

Please visit the Rotary.org, 'End Polio' page for more information.

BIBLIOGRAPHY

ANDREJEVIC, Mark. 2004. Reality TV: The Work of Being Watched. Maryland: Rowman and Littlefield Publishers, Inc. p. 8

BELL, Emma., 2008. From Bad Girl to Mad Girl. Genders Online Journal, [Online]. 48, part 3. Available at: http://www.genders.org/g48/g48_bell.html[Accessed on 08 February 2010].

BIRD, S. Elizabeth. 1997. What a Story! In J. Lull and S. Hinerman, eds. Media Scandals. Cambridge: Polity Press.

BORDO, Susan. 1993. Unbearable Weight: Feminism, Western Culture and the Body. Berkeley: University Of California Press. p. 192

CALINESCU, Matei. 1987. Five Faces of Modernity. Durham: Duke University Press. p. 134, 135.

CHANNEL 4. 2003. Big Brother Help [Online]. Available at: http://www.channel4.com/entertainment/tv/microsites/B/bb4/footer/help_4.html [Accessed on 07 February 2010].

CURRAN, James and GUREVITCH, Michael. 1996. Mass Media and Society (2nd ed). London: Arnold. p. 54

DELANEY, Sam. 18 January 2010. 'Media Guardian'. The Guardian [Online]. Available at: http://www.guardian.co.uk/media/2010/jan/18/sam-delaney-interview-heat [Accessed on 20 January 2010].

GAMSON, Joshua. 1994. Claims To Fame: Celebrity In Contemporary America. London: University Of California Press.

HAYWARD, K., Yar, M., 2006. The 'chav' phenomenon: Consumption, media and the construction of a new underclass. Crime, Media, Culture, [Online]. 2(1), p. 11. Available at: http://cmc.sagepub.com/cgi/content/abstract/2/1/9 [Accessed on 07 February 2010].

HILL, Annette. 2005. Reality TV: Audiences and Popular Factual Television. Oxon: Routledge.

HOLLOWS, Joanne. 2000. Feminism, femininity And Popular Culture. Manchester: Manchester University Press. p. 117.

JOHANSSON, S., 2008. Gossip, Sport and Pretty Girls. Journalism Practice, [Online]. 2(3), p. 402. Available at: http://dx.doi.org/10.1080/17512780802281131 [Accessed on 07 February 2010].

REYNOLDS, Mark. 19 March 2003. 'Entertainment'. London Evening Standard. Ex-Kitten was a howler [Online]. Available at: http://www.thisislondon. co.uk/news/article-3882712-ex-kitten-was-a howler.do [Accessed on 06 February 2010].

MARSHALL, P. David. 1997. Celebrity and Power: Fame in Contemporary Culture. Minneapolis: University of Minnesota Press. p. 121

MARX, Karl and ENGELS Friedrich. 1947. Ruling Class and Ruling Ideas. In C. J. Arthur, ed. The German Ideology. USA: International Publishers Co.,

MCGUIGAN, Jim. 1999. Modernity and Postmodern Culture (2nd ed). Berkshire: Open University Press.

MCQUAIL, Denis. 1983. Mass Communication Theory (4th ed). London: SAGE Publications.

METRO. 2007. Wedding Was A Sham [Online]. Available at: http://www.metro.co.uk/showbi z/42706-our-wedding-was-a-sham-says-brian-mcfadden [Accessed on 05 February 2010].

MOLE, T., 2008. Lord Byron and the End of Fame. International Journals of Cultural Studies, [Online]. 11(3), p. 347. Available at: http://ics.sagepub.com/ cgi/content/abstract/11/3/343 [Accessed on 07 February 2010].

MTV UK. 2009. Kerry Katona: What's The Problem [Online]. Available at: http://www.mtv.co.uk/ artists/kerry-katona [Accessed on 08 February 2010].

PRICE, Vincent. 1992. Public Opinion. California: SAGE Publications, Inc.

REDMOND, Sean and HOLMES, Su. 2007. Stardom and Celebrity: A Reader. London: Sage. p. 193

ROJEK, Chris. 2001. Celebrity. London: Reaktion Books Ltd.

TYLER, I., BENNETT, B., 2010. Celebrity Chav: Fame, Femininity and Social Class. European Journal of Cultural Studies, 13(3/4), p. 4.

FURTHER READING

BRAUDY, L. 1997. The Frenzy of Renown: Fame and Its History. New York: Vintage.

BRUNSDON, C., and SPIGEL, L. 2007. Feminist Television

Criticism (2 ed). Buckingham: Open University Press.

Culture and The Public Sphere by Jim McGuigan Routledge. London and New York. 1996.

Cyberspace Textuality: Computer Technology and Literary Theory Edited by Marie-Laurie Ryan Indiana University Press, Bloomington and Indianapolis 1999

CROTEAU, D. R., & HOYNES, W. 2002. Media/ Society: Industries, Images and Audiences (3rd ed). Thousand Oaks, California: Pine Forge Press.

ECO, U. 1979. Theory of Semiotics (Advances in Semiotics). Bloomington: Indiana University Press.

GREER, G. 1972. The Female Eunuch. New York: Bantam Books.

HEAT WORLD. 2010. Celebrity, Entertainment, Style & much more [Online} Available at: http://www.heatworld.com/ [Accessed on20 January 2010].

KORSCH, K. (1971). Marxism and Philosophy. London: Monthly Review Press.

Modernity and Postmodern Culture by Jim McGuigan Open University Press. 1999. Buckingham and Philadelphia

MCBRIDE, J. 1992. Frank Capra The Catastrophe of Success. New York: Touchstone.

MCGUIGAN, J. 1996. Culture and the Public Sphere (1 ed.). New York: Routledge.

THE SUN. 2010. The Best for News, Sport, Showbiz, Celebrities & TV [Online] Available at: http://www.thesun.co.uk/sol/homepage/[Accessed on 25 January 2010}.

The Handbook of New Media Edited by Leah A. Lievrouw and Sonia Livingstone Sage Publications 2006.

Media Theory: An Introduction by Fred Inglis Blackwell 1990.

Zero Comments: Blogging and Critical Internet Culture by Geert Lovink Routledge New York and London 2008.

ABOUT BERTHA MKWELELE

*B*ertha Mkwelele lives in British Columbia, Canada with her husband. She is the Executive Director and Co-Founder of the Neema Edward Mkwelele Wellness Foundation and an advocate for girls, especially those in her home country of Tanzania.

Media in the Celebrity Culture Sphere and Other Essays is Bertha Mkwelele's second book. It is a collection of written academic materials and essays left behind by her late daughter, Neema Edward Mkwelele along with reflective comment by Bertha.

Bertha wrote this book while she was still marketing *Nature is Unlimited Broadcasting Station: Flowers she wore on her feet,* a story about her daughter's life.

After Neema's memorial service, she came across academic materials and essays left behind by her daughter and she decided to become an audience in a unique way for the purpose of understanding what Neema wrote about the media information dissemination in general.

A big question for Bertha was, has the role of the media changed from when Neema was still a student? She wanted to compare contemporary interpretations of media's role with the interpretation Neema discussed in her essays.

Bertha could never have imaged that Neema's work was as exceptionally creative as it was. She found a world of discovery, inspiration, and the sense of possibility, the same things Neema herself would have voiced today if she had not so suddenly and tragically passed away.

Web:
www.neemaedwardmkwelelewellnessfoundation.org